CORPORATE
GOVERNANCE

Second
Edition

CORPORATE
GOVERNANCE

Kenneth A. Kim
State University of New York at Buffalo

John R. Nofsinger
Washington State University

PEARSON
Prentice
Hall

UPPER SADDLE RIVER, NEW JERSEY 07458

Library of Congress Cataloging-in-Publication Data

Kim, Kenneth A.
  Corporate governance / Kenneth A. Kim, John R. Nofsinger.—2nd ed.
    p. cm.
  ISBN 0-13-173534-9
  1. Corporate governance—United States. I. Nofsinger, John R. II. Title.

HD2741.K4713 2007
338.7'4—dc22

2006003612

AVP/Executive Editor: David Alexander
VP/Editorial Director: Jeff Shelstad
Manager, Product Development:
  Pam Hersperger
Project Manager: Francesca Calogero
Editorial Assistant: Michael Dittamo
Product Development Manager,
  Media: Nancy Welcher
AVP/Executive Marketing
  Manager: Sharon Koch
Senior Managing Editor,
  Production: Cynthia Regan

Production Editor: Melissa Feimer
Permissions Coordinator: Charles Morris
Manufacturing Buyer: Michelle Klein
Cover Design: Jayne Conte
Cover Illustration/Photo: Getty Images
Composition: Integra
Full-Service Project
  Management: Integra
Printer/Binder: R. R. Donnelley
Typeface: 10/12 TimesTen

Credits and acknowledgments borrowed from other sources and reproduced, with permission, in this textbook appear on appropriate page within text.

Pearson Education LTD.
Pearson Education Singapore, Pte. Ltd
Pearson Education, Canada, Ltd
Pearson Education—Japan

Pearson Education Australia PTY, Limited
Pearson Education North Asia Ltd
Pearson Educación de Mexico, S. A. de C. V.
Pearson Education Malaysia, Pte. Ltd.

10 9 8 7 6
ISBN 0-13-173534-9

Contents

Preface

Corporate Governance, 2nd edition, is the perfect text to supplement:

a) any corporate finance class;
b) an accounting class;
c) a variety of management courses such as strategy, ethics, and/or especially business and society; and
d) a business law class.

In addition, this text is sufficiently self-contained so that it can be used as the sole text in a business administration module specifically focusing on corporate governance. The book can also be used for executive training programs and to this end can serve as an important reference for executive and academic libraries.

A decade ago, the term "corporate governance" was largely academic jargon. Today, the term is familiar to almost everyone. Unfortunately, its familiarity in our society comes about because of revelations of one shocking corporate scandal after another: executives caught pilfering from their firms; accountants helping companies doctor their financial numbers; analysts irresponsibly hyping internet stocks. Meanwhile, boards of directors, lenders and credit rating agencies, shareholder activists, and regulators seemed almost absent or ineffective in staving off the crisis. The market lapsed into a meltdown during the early 2000s. With investor confidence down, and with the flaws of our corporate governance system revealed, everyone responded with calls for regulatory reform and corporate governance improvements.

Why is corporate governance important? The goal of every firm is to increase its shareholders' wealth. However, the firm's value diminishes when it does not have the trust of its shareholders. Without the trust of investors, firms will not be able to obtain new capital and grow. *The entire economy suffers when trust is broken.* Effective corporate governance can instill confidence, and thus trust, in our companies and markets.

Believe it or not, we already have an extensive system of corporate governance. The system has never been perfect but we have only begun to notice that. Now the media regularly discusses corporate governance. Business and law schools have begun incorporating the topic of corporate governance into the classrooms and curriculum.

HIGHLIGHTS

In **Chapter 1**, we provide an overview of the U.S. corporation. Then we lay out the reasons why effective corporate governance is needed. In general, we believe that there are many mechanisms in which corporations can be effectively monitored.

After Chapter 1, the **rest of the book** is organized into chapters that discuss **each** corporate governance mechanism.

Every chapter is organized in the same way, and each chapter is self-contained. Each chapter begins with a detailed overview of the monitor or monitoring mechanism, and then highlights potential problems.

In every chapter, **real world examples** are used to illustrate the outlined problems.

Every chapter provides an **international perspective**, and a **list of websites** so that students can have access to the latest developments in corporate governance.

At the end of each chapter, we provide **Review Questions** that are based on the chapter reading, and **Discussion Questions** that can facility class discussions. We also offer **Exercises** that students can do to further their understanding of the chapter material. Lastly, we provide **Exercises for non-U.S. Students** to help them dig into corporate governance in their own country.

NEW TO THIS EDITION

- Three brand new chapters!
  - **Chapter 8 – Corporate Takeovers**: Discusses how poorly performing companies are taken over by other companies.
  - **Chapter 10 – New Governance Rules**: Provides a summary and discussion of the new corporate governance regulations.
  - **Chapter 11 – Corporate Citizenship**: Focuses on the modern evolution of the stakeholder view of the firm, called corporate social responsibility or corporate citizenship.
- The "Investment Banks" and the "Financial Analysts" chapters are now combined into *one chapter*, which includes a discussion on the result of SEC investigations into analyst bias and investment bank incentives (Chapter 5 – Investment Banks and Securities Analysts).
- Now includes a discussion on the creditor as a monitor – how banks monitor the firms that they lend to (Chapter 6 – Creditors and Credit Rating Agencies).

FOR INSTRUCTORS

The following supplements are available to adopting instructors. For detailed descriptions, please visit: www.prenhall.com/nofsinger

Instructor's Resource Center (IRC) online: Login at www.prenhall.com/irc.
PowerPoint slides (created by the authors): Visit the IRC for this text.

INSTRUCTOR'S RESOURCE CENTER

Register. Redeem. Login.

www.prenhall.com/irc is where instructors can access a variety of print, media, and presentation resources available with this text in downloadable, digital format. For most texts, resources are also available for course management platforms, such as Blackboard, WebCT, and Course Compass.

It gets better. Once you register, you will not have additional forms to fill out, or multiple usernames and passwords to remember to access new titles and/or editions. As a registered faculty member, you can login directly to download resource files, and receive immediate access and instructions for installing Course Management content to your campus server.

Need help? Our dedicated Technical Support team is ready to assist instructors with questions about the media supplements that accompany this text. Visit: http://247.prenhall.com/ for answers to frequently-asked questions and toll-free user support phone numbers.

ACKNOWLEDGMENTS

This book could not have been written without the guidance and support that we have received from many people throughout our careers. We acknowledge all of our former teachers and professional colleagues, and our former and current research collaborators, for shaping the way we think about corporate governance. We also readily acknowledge our friends who continue to work in the "real world" as they keep us grounded in reality, thus preventing us from getting carried away with our theories. We also appreciate our former students for letting us "try out" most of the material used in this textbook in our own classrooms. We appreciate our publisher, Prentice Hall (especially Francesca Calogero), for working with us, and for all of the reviewers that have given us such valuable feedback for both editions:

Tim Michael–University of Houston Clear Lake
Betty Simkins–Oklahoma State University
Curt H. Stiles–University of North Carolina at Wilmington
Diane Swanson–Kansas State University
Melissa Williams–University of Houston Clear Lake

Finally, we are deeply indebted to our close friends and family for their support. They help us maintain our sanity.

FEEDBACK

The author and product team would appreciate hearing from you! Let us know what you think about this book by writing to college_finance@prenhall.com. Please include "Feedback about Kim/Nofsinger 2e" in the subject line.

You can also contact the author team directly. They would also be happy to receive your comments and questions:

Ken Kim–kk52@buffalo.edu.
John Nofsinger–john_nofsinger@wsu.edu.

If you have questions related to this product, please contact our customer service department online at www.247.prenhall.com.

About The Authors

Kenneth A. Kim, Ph.D., is a finance professor at the State University of New York (SUNY) at Buffalo. Kim recently served as the corporate governance consultant to the CFA Institute on its "body of knowledge" pertaining to its CFA programs. During 1998 and 1999, he worked as a financial economist at the U.S. Securities and Exchange Commission in Washington, DC, where he worked on a wide variety of corporate finance and governance issues, including Mergers & Acquisitions regulations. His primary research interests include corporate finance, corporate governance, and behavioral finance. He has been published in the *Journal of Finance*, the *Journal of Business*, the *Journal of Corporate Finance*, and the *Journal of Banking and Finance*, among other leading journals. Kim is a co-author of *Infectious Greed* and the textbook, *Global Corporate Finance*.

John R. Nofsinger, Ph.D., is a finance professor, and Lang Fellow, at Washington State University and author of *Investment Madness, The Psychology of Investing, Investment Blunders*, and coauthor of *Infectious Greed*. Widely acknowledged as one of the world's leading experts in investor psychology and behavioral finance, he is frequently quoted in financial media including the *Wall Street Journal, Fortune, BusinessWeek, SmartMoney, Bloomberg,* and *CNBC,* as well as other media from the *Washington Post to Wired.com.* Nofsinger has published more than 20 articles in leading scholarly and professional journals. His research has won awards at the Financial Management Association, Chicago Quantitative Alliance, and PACAP conferences. He has also done advanced research for the New York Stock Exchange and the Association for Investment Management and Research.

1

CORPORATIONS AND CORPORATE GOVERNANCE

Capitalism is an economic system of business based on private enterprise. Individuals and businesses own land, farms, factories, and equipment, and they use those assets in an attempt to earn profits. Capitalism is a good economic system because it can provide rewards for those who work hard and who are inventive and creative enough to figure out new or improved products and services. One potential reward for creating value in an economy is the accumulation of personal wealth. The wealth incentive provides the fuel to generate new ideas and to foster economic value that provides jobs and raises our standard of living.

The main goal of a company is to create an environment conducive to earning long-term profits, which stem from two main sources. First, a business must provide products and/or services to a customer base. A large portion of a firm's value derives from the current and future profits of its business activity. Finding ways to increase profits from core operations can increase economic value. Second, increased profits can come from growth in the sales of an existing product or sales resulting from the introduction of a new product.

Expansion usually requires additional money, or capital. Business activities also entail risk. The abilities to access capital and to control risk are important in the success or failure of a firm. Such abilities are influenced by the manner in which a firm is organized. In this chapter, we first describe different forms of business, with emphasis on the corporation. We then describe the people involved in the corporate form of business, and the separation of owners and managers that this entails. This separation is problematic, and we describe how corporate governance can address this problem.

FORMS OF BUSINESS OWNERSHIP

In general, a business can be a sole proprietorship, a partnership, or a corporation. Other forms exist,[1] but we will focus on these three as this is the most general distinction. Each organizational form involves different advantages and

1

disadvantages. A **sole proprietorship** is a business owned by a single person. These businesses are relatively easy to start up and business tax is computed at the personal level. Due to its simplicity, sole proprietorships are ubiquitous, representing more than 70 percent of all U.S. businesses.[2] However, there are several significant drawbacks. Such firms often have a limited lifespan (they die with the owner's death or retirement), they have a limited ability to obtain capital, and the owner bears unlimited personal liability for the firm.

A **partnership** is similar to a sole proprietorship but there is more than one owner. As such, a partnership shares the advantages and disadvantages of the sole proprietorship. While one obvious advantage of a partnership is the ability to pool capital, this advantage may not be as important as combining service-oriented expertise and skill, especially for larger partnerships. Examples of such partnerships include accounting firms, law firms, investment banks, and advertising firms.

This book focuses on the third business form, the **corporation**. Fewer than 20 percent of all U.S. businesses are corporations but they generate approximately 90 percent of the country's business revenue.[3] The corporation is its own legal entity, as if it were a person. For example, the corporation can engage in business transactions and other business activities in its own name. Corporate officers act as agents for the firm and authorize those activities.

Perhaps the most important advantage of the corporate business form is access to capital markets. Public companies can raise money by issuing stocks and bonds to investors. While sole proprietorships and partnerships may access millions of dollars through the business owners' wealth and through banks, corporations may be able to access billions of dollars. Access to this capital causes entrepreneurs such as Bill Gates of Microsoft, Steve Jobs of Apple, and Larry Ellison of Oracle, to take their companies public so that their businesses can become corporations. To raise money for expansion in the capital markets, the business sells stock to investors.

For example, between 1977 and 1980, Apple Computer sold a total of 121,000 computers. To meet the potential demand for millions of computers per year, Apple needed to expand operations significantly. As a result, in 1980 Apple became a public corporation and sold $65 million worth of stock. Steve Jobs, cofounder of Apple, still owned more shares than anyone else, but he owned less than half of the firm. He gave up a great deal of ownership to new investors in exchange for the capital to expand the firm. (Incidentally, as we will describe later, this decision would later come back to haunt Jobs.)

Stockholders, or shareholders, are the owners of a public corporation. These shareholders receive any value that is created by the firm, but they can also lose their investments if the firm goes bankrupt. The process has two benefits. First, any individual, as long as she has some money, can invest in business and increase her wealth over the long term. Second, businesses with growth potential can obtain the capital needed to expand, which creates economic value, jobs, and taxes. A corporation has an infinite life unless terminated by bankruptcy or merger with another firm. The owners of corporations enjoy limited financial liability because they can lose only, at most, the value of their ownership shares. Further, corporate ownership is usually liquid, and ownership stakes can be easily bought and sold as stocks in a marketplace, such as the New York Stock Exchange (NYSE) or NASDAQ.

The advantages of the corporate business form are appealing, but there are also major disadvantages. Corporate profits are subject to business taxes before any income goes to shareholders in the form of dividends. Subsequently, shareholders must also pay personal taxes on dividend income. Therefore, shareholders are exposed to double taxation. In addition, running a corporation can be expensive. For example, the costs of hiring accountants and legal experts, the costs of communicating with all shareholders, the costs of complying with regulations, and so forth, can cost millions of dollars per year. Finally, and perhaps the most important disadvantage, corporations suffer from potentially serious governance problems. Most investors only own a small stake of a large public corporation, so they consequently do not feel any true sense of ownership or control over the firms in which they own stock.

SEPARATION OF OWNERSHIP AND CONTROL

In 1932, Adolf Berle and Gardiner Means wrote what was to become a famous book about the corporate form of business.[4] They pointed out that corporations were becoming so large that the ownership and control was separated. The stockholders own the firm and officers (or executives) control the firm. This situation comes about because the thousands, or even hundreds of thousands, of investors who own public firms could not collectively make the daily decisions needed to operate a business. Firms hire managers for that work.

Most shareholders do not wish to take part in a firm's business activities. These shareholders act like passive investors, not active owners. The difference is subtle but important. Owners focus on the business performance of the firm and investors focus on the risk and return of their stock portfolios. While diversifying reduces risk for the investor, ownership of many companies also makes participation and influence in those companies less likely. Therefore, investors tend to be inactive shareholders of many firms.

There is a problem with this separation of ownership and control. Why would the managers care about the owners? Berle and Means pointed out that with managers being freed from vigilant owners, they would only pursue enough profit to keep stockholders satisfied while they sought self-serving gratification in the form of perks, power, and/or fame. In academic terms, this situation is known as the **principal-agent problem** or the **agency problem**. The owners are the principal and the manager is the agent who is supposed to work for the owner. If shareholders cannot effectively monitor the managers' behavior, then managers may be tempted to use the firm's assets for their own ends, all at the expense of shareholders. This should not be hard to imagine. Secretaries may take home office supplies. When traveling, mid-level managers may order as much food as allowed on their expense accounts. Executives might prefer fancy oak furniture for their offices and the use of corporate jets when traveling. All of these actions are at the expense of shareholders. If people feel they can get away with these minor offenses, what else might they try?

Among all employees, the ones who have the greatest ability to steal from shareholders the most are the executives. They have the most power and control in the corporation. Mid-level managers have bosses who look at expense reports. Who watches the executives? If executives have temptations, and if executives are not watched by engaged owners, then we have a serious problem.

Solutions to this problem tend to come in two categories, incentives and monitoring. The incentive solution is to tie the wealth of the executive to the wealth of the shareholders, so that executives and shareholders want the same thing. This is called aligning executive incentives with shareholder desires. Managers would then act and behave in a way that is also best for the other shareholders. How can this be done? For most U.S. companies, executives are given stock, restricted stock, stock options, or combinations as a significant component of their compensation. The advantages and disadvantages of this incentive solution are explored in the next chapter. Suffice it to say, there are troubles with this solution to the agency problem.

The second solution is to set up mechanisms for monitoring the behavior of managers. Several monitoring mechanisms are discussed shortly in this chapter, and they are importantly discussed throughout this book.

CAN INVESTORS INFLUENCE MANAGERS?

Theoretically, managers work for owners (shareholders). In reality, because shareholders are usually inactive, the firm actually seems to belong to management. Some active shareholders have tried to influence management, but they are often met with defeat. Recent evidence of unsuccessful outcomes of shareholder proposals is quite telling. Shareholders have the power to make proposals that can be voted on at the annual shareholders meeting. There are generally two types of proposals, those related to governance (e.g. suggesting changes in board structure) and those oriented to social reform (e.g. proposing to stop selling chemicals to rogue countries). About half of all shareholder-initiated proposals progress far enough in the process to reach the voting stage. When there is a vote, such proposals usually are defeated.[5]

A huge factor in whether a proposal is successful depends on management's opinion. Without management approval, proposals have little chance of succeeding. Traditionally, shareholders have trusted management to know what is best for the firm. Most shareholders will go along with whatever management wants.

Monitors
Generally speaking, the investing public does not know what goes on at the firm's operational level. Managers handle day-to-day operations, and they know that their work is mostly unknown to investors. Consequently, managers may not act in the shareholder's best interest, which demonstrates the need for monitors.

EXAMPLE 1.1

CARLY FIORINA'S TAKEOVER OF COMPAQ

For an illustration of management control and influence, consider the 2002 merger between Hewlett-Packard (HP) and Compaq.[6] Carly Fiorina, the Hewlett-Packard CEO, announced on September 4, 2001, that HP would acquire Compaq for $25.5 billion. The stock markets, industry experts, and the business media reacted negatively to the news. Hewlett-Packard stock was down 18 percent following the announcement, and even Compaq's stock declined by 10 percent, which is rare for a target firm. Of particular note, David W. Packard and Walter Hewlett, both significant shareholders (when including the Packard Foundation, the pair owned 18 percent of HP stock) and sons of HP's founders, were also strongly opposed to the acquisition. In fact, they took out newspaper ads asking other HP shareholders to vote against the merger.

However, Fiorina went ahead with her plan, despite attacks from both Packard and Hewlett, and on March 19, 2002, most of the other shareholders voted in favor of the acquisition. Despite the controversy and the drop in stock prices, most shareholders voted with management's wishes and approved the acquisition. This example reinforces the idea that even though some investors may want to influence business strategy and direction, management controls the firm.

Figure 1.1 illustrates the separation of ownership and control between stockholders and managers. In addition, the figure shows that monitors exist inside the corporate structure, outside the structure, and in government.

The monitors inside a public firm are the board of directors who oversee management and are supposed to represent shareholders' interests. The board evaluates management and can also design compensation contracts to tie management's salaries to the firm's performance. You may remember that Apple Computer was cofounded by Steve Jobs. When the firm became a public corporation, Jobs was the largest shareholder, and he also became CEO. However, the Apple board of directors felt that Jobs was not experienced enough to steer the firm through its rapid expansion. Therefore, they hired John Sculley as CEO in 1983. In 1985, a power struggle ensued for control of the firm, and the board backed Sculley. Jobs was forced out of Apple and no longer had a say in business operations even though he was the largest shareholder. (Interestingly, when Apple Computer experienced difficulties in the late 1990s, the board hired Jobs back as CEO!)

As shown in the figure, outsiders—including auditors, analysts, investment banks, credit rating agencies, and outside legal counsel—all interact with the firm and monitor manager activities. Auditors examine the firm's accounting systems

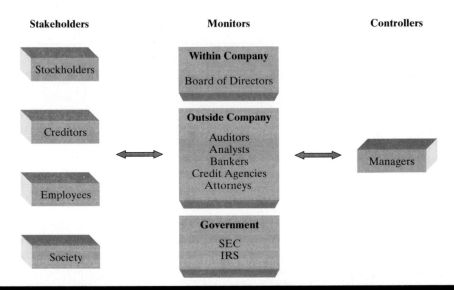

FIGURE 1.1 Separation of Ownership, Monitoring, and Control

and comment on whether financial statements fairly represent the financial position of the firm. Investors and other stakeholders use the public financial statements to make decisions about the firm's financial health, prospects, performance, and value. Even though investors may not have the ability or opportunity to validate the firm's activities, accountants and auditors can attest to the firm's financial health and verify its activities.

Investment analysts who follow a firm conduct their own, independent evaluations of the company's business activities and report their findings to the investment community. Analysts are supposed to give unbiased and expert assessments. Investment banks also interact with management by helping firms access the capital markets. When obtaining more capital from public investors, firms must register documents with regulators that show potential investors the condition of the firm. Investment banks help firms with this process and advise managers on how to interact with the capital markets.

The government also monitors business activities through the Securities and Exchange Commission (SEC) and the Internal Revenue Service (IRS). The SEC regulates public firms for the protection of public investors, and it makes policy and prosecutes violators in civil courts. However, for criminal prosecution the SEC must turn to the U.S. Justice Department. The IRS enforces the tax rules to ensure corporations pay taxes, just as it does with individual U.S. citizens.

In response to the corporate and investment community scandals, the U.S. government responded with the enactment of the Sarbanes-Oxley Act of 2002. Overall, the Act created a new oversight body to regulate auditors, created laws pertaining to corporate responsibility, and increased punishments for corporate white-collar crime. Both the NYSE and NASDAQ developed and adopted their own governance-focused listing standards to address the problems.

Market forces can also help discipline management. If a manager is not doing a good job, either because he is bad at managing or because he is abusing his managerial discretion, then his firm might get taken over and he is subsequently fired. In this sense, the fear of a potential takeover might represent a powerful disciplinary mechanism to make sure that managers perform to the best of their abilities and to make sure that managerial discretion is controlled.

Stakeholders also monitor the firm. Some stockholders, such as large institutional investors like pension funds, are active monitors. Creditors will make sure the firm can handle its debt. Employees, such as internal auditors, might monitor the firm to make sure it is healthy. And society could instill a sense of corporate citizenship to the firm so that firm executives feel a sense of responsibility toward their community.

As a group, this is a pretty impressive set of monitors. Unfortunately, all of these mechanisms can fail at one time or another. An important purpose of this book is to describe each of these corporate monitors and the problems that may exist with each of them.

AN INTEGRATED SYSTEM OF GOVERNANCE

The corporate governance system is integrated and complicated. The potential incentives for executives, auditors, boards, banks, and so on, to misbehave are intertwined. By focusing on one part of the system, readers might not fully understand how the governance system can break down. Consider the diagram of corporate participants in Figure 1.2. The arrows show the relationships between the groups. Note that these relationships are interconnected.

For example, analysts talk to management to gauge the prospects of the firm. Managers want to paint a rosy picture so that analysts will recommend a "buy" rating and the stock price will rise. However, this situation may also cause analysts to predict a high profit forecast for the company, and the managers may struggle to meet the high forecast. If the business activities of the firm do not

FIGURE 1.2 Interlinking Relationships among Business Participants

merit the high profit forecast, managers might then pressure their accounting department to help. In some cases, consultants are hired who recommend aggressive accounting techniques to help show increased profits.

The public auditors for the firm may have had a long and fruitful relationship with the company, auditing the books for many years. The auditors are proud to have a prestigious corporation as a client and do not want to end this relationship; consequently they may not press too hard on limiting aggressive accounting methods. Why are managers so obsessed with pushing hard for smooth and increasing profits? Why are they obsessed with gaining analyst favor? It is because a board (which is largely picked by the managers) awards them stock options and stock incentives. If managers can increase the price of the stock, then they can cash in their options and stock and become rich.

Regulators also monitor managers' behavior. However, regulators often have experience as partners in consulting firms, auditing firms, or law firms that are an integral part of the system. By participating in the corporate system, regulators know how it works. Unfortunately, they might also have their own conflicts of interest.

This book describes the following monitors or monitoring mechansims:

- incentive contracts that supposedly align executive incentives with shareholder interests;
- accountants and auditors who check the firm's financial statements;
- boards of directors who represent shareholders;
- investment banks and analysts that brings securities to the public for sale and evaluates them;
- creditors and credit rating agencies who monitor the firm's ability to handle debt;
- shareholders themselves;
- the corporate takeover market where supposedly good firms take over bad firms;
- the Securities and Exchange Comission who are the official regulators of the securities industry;
- new governance laws; and
- corporate citizenship that should instill a sense of corporate responsibility to the executives.

INTERNATIONAL MONITORING

Other capitalist countries use the types of monitoring and incentives used in the U.S. to align the interests of executives and shareholders. However, important differences do occur. Some countries use different compensation contracts and have different accounting standards. Many countries do not have the same institutional investing environment as the U.S. Some countries are bank-oriented rather than capital markets-oriented. A country's legal environment can explain some of the differences. However, corporate scandals can occur in every country. In this book, every chapter contains an international perspective on that chapter's topic.

Summary

The corporate form of business allows firms that need capital to obtain it and expand, thereby helping the economy. This form also allows people with money to provide those funds and profit from having ownership in business. The disadvantage of public corporations lies in the relation between ownership and control. Managers who control the firm can take advantage of the investors who own the firm. To inhibit poor managerial behavior, shareholders try to align the executives' interests with their own interests through incentive programs involving stock and stock options. In addition, the corporate system has several different groups of people that monitor managers. Unfortunately, both alignment incentives and monitoring groups bring to the table their own set of problems. The corporate system has interrelated incentives that combine to create an environment where people might act unethically. The following chapters discuss each aspect of the incentive and monitor system of corporate governance.

Review Questions

1. What are the three basic forms of business ownership? What are the advantages and disadvantages to each?
2. How can executive compensation align manager interests with shareholder interests?
3. Name and describe the different groups that monitor a firm.
4. Describe the separation of ownership and control. Explain how that separation comes about and why it leads to problems.

Discussion Questions

1. Figure 1.1. shows monitors and stakeholders. In your opinion, which group is in the best position to monitor the firm? Explain why. Which group has the potential to be the weakest monitor? Explain why.
2. Figure 1.2 shows how business participants are interlinked. In your opinion, which links potentially create the greatest problems for stockholders? Explain why.
3. In your opinion, how do you think U.S. corporations became as important and as large as they are today?
4. In general, and in your personal experience, which has been the most effective way to get people to do what you want:
   (i) provide incentives for good behavior;
   (ii) closely monitor them; or
   (iii) give punishments for bad behavior?

From what you have seen, read, and heard from the mass media, journalists, politicians, etc., what do these people think is the best way to get executives to behave ethically? If your answers to these two questions are different, then try to reconcile the differences.

Exercises

1. This chapter described how Carly Fiorina exerted control over Hewlitt-Packard despite objections from large shareholders. Find another example of how management went against shareholders' wishes and describe what happened.
2. Do some research and explain how U.S. corporations became as important and as large as they are today. Some academics have discussed the "theory of the firm" or the "nature of the firm." To what extent, and how, do these theories explain U.S. corporations today. How do agency problems play a role in these theories?

Exercises for Non-U.S. Students

1. Figure 1.2 shows how business participants are interlinked in the U.S. Create a figure showing the inter-linkages among business participants in your country. Explain the interlinkages.
2. How severe is the agency problem in your country? Explain. Also, provide real examples.
3. In your country, which ideology seems to be used in resolving agency conflicts:

   (i) provide incentives to executives for good behavior;
   (ii) closely monitor the executives; or
   (iii) give punishments to executives for bad behavior?

   Do you think it is working? Explain why or why not.

Endnotes

1. There are many hybrid forms of business organization, such as the Limited Liability Corporation. While this book is about the public corporation, comparisons to simple forms of business, such as sole proprietorships and partnerships illustrate the characteristics of corporate ownership and control.
2. William J. Megginson, *Corporate Finance Theory* (Reading, MA: Addison-Wesley, 1997), p. 40.
3. William J. Megginson, *Corporate Finance Theory* (Reading, MA: Addison-Wesley, 1997), p. 40.
4. Adolf Berle and Gardiner Means, *The Modern Corporation and Private Property* (New York, MacMillion, 1932).
5. See, for example, Stuart Gillan and Laura Starks, "A Survey of Shareholder Activism: Motivation and Empirical Evidence," *Contemporary Finance Digest* 2, no. 3 (1998):10–34; Cynthia Campbell, Stuart Gillan, and Cathy Niden, "Current Perspectives on Shareholder Proposals: Lessons from the 1997 Proxy Season," Financial Management 28, no. 1 (1999):89–98; and Gordon and Pound, "Information, Ownership Structure, and Shareholder Voting: Evidence from Shareholder-Sponsored Corporate Governance Proposals," *Journal of Finance* 47, no. 2 (1993):697–718.
6. Larry Magid, "Many Would Lose in Hewlett-Packard, Compaq Merger," *Los Angeles Times,* www.larrysworld.com/articles/synd.hpmerger.htm: Mike Elgan and Susan B. Shor, "Gloves Are Off in Merger Fight," *HP World* 5, no. 2, www.interex.org/hpworldnews/hpw202/01news.html.

CHAPTER

2

EXECUTIVE INCENTIVES

A corporation's ownership and control are separated between two parties—stockholders and officers. The stockholders own the firm and officers (or executives) control the firm. A simple problem exists with this separation of ownership and control. Why should the managers care about the owners? Managers may put personal interests first, even at the expense of owners. This situation is known as the **principal-agent problem** or the **agency problem**. The shareholders of a corporation are the principals and the managers who run the company are the agents. If shareholders cannot effectively monitor managers' behavior, then the latter may be tempted to use the firm's assets to enhance their own lifestyles.

Solutions to agency problems tend to fall in two categories: incentives and monitoring. The board of directors, auditors, and other components of the governance system serve to monitor managers; this is discussed in later chapters. The incentive solution, covered in this chapter, ties an executive's wealth to the wealth of shareholders so that everyone shares the same goal. This is called aligning executive incentives with shareholders' desires. Managers should then act in ways that also benefit other shareholders. To align manager and shareholder interests, most executives receive stock options as a significant component of their compensation. In this chapter, we focus on the incentives of modern executive compensation.

POTENTIAL MANAGERIAL TEMPTATIONS

A manager has a variety of stakeholders that are affected by his actions. These include investors such as stockholders (owners) and lenders, the firm's customers and suppliers, the firm's employees, and of course himself. A good manager should put the needs of other stakeholders before his own but human nature may cause him to put his needs first. Examples of self-serving managerial actions include:

- shirking (i.e. not working hard);
- hiring friends;

- consuming excessive perks (e.g. purchasing extravagent office furniture, using company cars, enjoying large expense accounts);
- building empires (i.e. making the firm as large as possible even, though it may hurt the firm's per share value);
- taking no risks or chances to avoid being fired; and
- having a short-run horizon if the manager is near retirement.

One way to make sure that managers will not behave in these ways is to give them the right monetary incentives to act in the interests of their other stakeholders. We discuss various types of executive compensation that are aimed at accomplishing this task.

TYPES OF EXECUTIVE COMPENSATION

Company executives are compensated in many different ways. They receive a basic salary that also includes pension contributions and perquisites (company car, club memberships, and so on). In addition, top executives might receive a bonus that is usually linked to accounting-based performance measures. Lastly, managers might receive additional wealth through long-term incentive programs, usually in the form of stock options, which reward the manager for increasing the company's stock price. Stock grants are another common form of long-term awards.

Base Salary and Bonus

As with most jobs, CEOs are promised a specific annual salary. The base salary of a company CEO is often determined through the benchmarking method, which surveys peer CEO salaries for comparison.[1] Salaries less than the 50th percentile are considered under market, while salaries in the 50th to 75th percentile are competitive. CEO base salary has continuously drifted upward because CEOs typically argue for competitive salaries. So each year we often see CEOs getting nice raises and also we see new CEOs making more than current CEOs. Interestingly, this basic pay results more from characteristics of the firm (e.g. industry, size) than on characteristics of the CEO (e.g. age, experience). So a CEO of a large firm often gets a salary higher than a CEO of a smaller firm, regardless of the person's past success, age, and experience. Mercer Human Resource Consulting, in conjunction with the *Wall Street Journal*, annually surveys proxy statements for 350 of the largest U.S. companies to examine CEO compensation trends.[2] In 2004, the median base salary for CEOs of these large firms has been about $975,000.

At the end of every year, CEOs often receive cash bonuses. The size of the payment is based on the performance of the firm over the past year and is typically based on the accounting profit measurements of earnings per share (EPS) and earnings before interest and taxes (EBIT). Measures of economic value added (or EVA) are also common. These value-added measures are usually variations on earnings minus the cost of capital. The idea is to measure the value added to the firm in relation to the firm's costs of using different sources of money to conduct its business activities. Whether EBIT or EVA is used, a low threshold needs to be reached in order to qualify the CEO for a bonus. Higher levels of firm performance merit higher bonus amounts up to a specific maximum or cap. An advantage of awarding bonuses, as opposed to giving large raises, is that bonuses are one-time rewards for past *realized* performance, while raises are permanent additions to salaries for future unrealized performance. For these reasons, bonuses are a popular component of the overall compensation package. The median bonus payment for CEOs in large firms was about $1.5 million in 2004.

Stock Options

Executive stock options are the most common form of market-oriented incentive pay. Stock options are contracts that allow executives to buy shares of stock at a fixed price, called the exercise or strike price. Therefore, if the price of the stock rises above the strike price, the executive will capture the difference as a profit. For example, if the stock of a company trades at $50 per share, the CEO may be given options with a strike price at $50. Over the next few years, if the stock price rises to $75 per share, then shareholders would receive a 50 percent return on their stockholdings. The CEO could buy stock for $50 per share by exercising the option and sell it for $75 per share, thus making a $25 profit on each option owned. If the executive has options for 1 million shares, then he could pocket $25 million. If the stock price reaches $100 per share, the executive could cash in for $50 million. In contrast, if the stock price were to drop to less than $50 per share, then the options have no exercisable value and are said to be underwater. Executives treat stock options as compensation; they nearly always exercise the options to buy the stock and then sell the stock for the cash. Only rarely will an executive keep the stock.

Stock options give the executives of the firm the incentive to manage the firm in such a way that the stock price increases, which is precisely what the stockholders want as well. Therefore, stock options are believed to align managers' goals with shareholders' goals. This alignment helps to overcome some of the problems with the separation of ownership and control. The typical executive option contract assigns the strike price of the options to the prevailing stock price when the option is granted. The most common length of the options contract is 10 years. That is, the CEO has 10 years to increase the price of the stock and exercise the options. After 10 years the options expire. Executives cannot sell or transfer their options and are discouraged from hedging the stock price risk. The median option-based award realized for CEOs in large firms was $2.7 million in 2004. Executive stock options were not common prior to 1980.

Options and Accounting

The popularity of stock options as incentive compensation in the U.S. partly came from its favorable tax treatment for both the executive and the company. When options were granted, the company only needed to report an accounting cost when the strike price was less than the current stock price. Then the cost was amortized over the life of the option. Because most options were granted with

EXAMPLE 2.1

TEN HIGHEST PAID CEOs IN 2004 (INCLUDES SALARY, BONUS, AND STOCK OPTION GRANTS)

Terry Semel, Yahoo Inc.	$109,301,385	Dwight Schar, NVR Inc.	$51,058,500
Steven Jobs, Apple Computer	$86,315,789	Bruce Karatz, KB Home	$47,288,228
Lew Frankfort, Coach Inc.	$64,918,520	Robert Toll, Toll Brothers	$44,240,611
John Wilder, TXU Corp.	$54,960,893	Paul Evanson, Allegheny Energy	$40,543,354
Ray R. Irani, Occidential Petroleum	$52,648,142	Edward Zander, Motorola Inc.	$38,851,374

Source: www.aflcio.org/corporatewatch/

the strike price equal to the current stock price, the firm never had to report an accounting cost. Also, the manager can pick the year in which she will exercise the options and thus determine when the tax liability occurs. In addition, the compensation was and still is treated as a capital gain, not as income, which is an advantage to the CEO because capital gains taxes are lower than regular personal income taxes.

If an executive cashes in for $100 million, this cost does not appear on the firm's income statement; the firm does not have to report an accounting cost. However, the economic cost to the firm is real. Consider this simple example. A firm has 100 million shares outstanding and has given the executives options for 10 million shares. The firm currently has earnings of $100 million, or $1 per share. If the executives exercise their options, then they would buy 10 million shares from the firm at the strike price and sell them on the stock market. At that point, there would be 110 million shares outstanding, which means that the $100 million in earnings becomes only $0.91 per share. The earnings per share have fallen by 9 percent and the firm has become less profitable to its shareholders.

Since July 2005, firms are now required to expense executive stock options (this is referred to as FAS 123(R)). Even though stock options may have exercise prices at or below the current stock price when they are granted, they are still valuable. This value, which is estimated using a variation of a formula known as the Black-Scholes option pricing model, is now required to be deducted from reported income. This new regulation will make the granting of executive stock options less attractive. We discuss this regulation in more detail later in this chapter.

Stock Grants

Because of the perception that executive options may have contributed to the governance failures in the late 1990s and early 2000s, many companies have been looking for alternative forms of long-term incentive compensation. Two types have gained in popularity; restricted stock grants and performance shares.

Restricted stock is common stock of the company that includes a limitation that requires a certain length of time to pass or a certain goal to be achieved before the stock can be sold. Executives may receive a grant of shares that require 10 years to pass before the executive may sell them. Restricted stock has an advantage over options in that it's value does not go to zero when the stock price falls. Therefore, it does not have the asymmetric incentives that options cause. (Options are asymmetric because their exercisable value could end up being worth a lot or worth nothing.) Restricted stock grants have increased from 12 percent of total long-term incentives in 2002 to 23 percent in 2004. The median restricted stock grant for CEOs of large companies in 2004 was just over $1 million.

Performance shares refer to a company's stock given to executives only if certain performance criteria are met, such as earnings per share targets. In one sense, these shares could be viewed as bonuses for past realized performance. If the firm's stock price has increased, then these performance shares are more valuable to the CEO when he receives them. Performance share plans increased to 20 percent of the long-term incentive pay mix in 2004 and was just shy of $1 million for CEOs of large firms.

DOES INCENTIVE-BASED COMPENSATION WORK IN GENERAL?

There are two ways to examine whether or not incentive-based compensation works. First, one could try to see if there is a positive relation between firm performance and management compensation. This would be defined as *ex post* evidence. In other words, have managers been properly rewarded for increasing the firms' value? If the answer is yes, then we could surmise that incentive compensation works. Professors Michael Jensen and Kevin Murphy provide the most well-known evidence that the answer is pretty much "no."[3] They examined the total compensation of over 2,000 CEOs and they found that when the value of the firm increased by $1,000, then those CEOs were paid $3.25 more on average. Imagine a CEO who takes over a large firm. This CEO would have to increase the firm's value by over $300 million to increase their compensation by a mere $1 million. In academic jargon, we would say that the pay-for-performance sensitivity is very low.

Another way to assess the efficacy of incentive-based compensation is to see if those firms that enacted these compensation mechanisms subsequently experienced superior performance. This could be defined as *ex ante* evidence. In other words, once managers are given incentives, then did the firms subsequently perform well? Intuitively we might expect the answer to be "yes" but surprisingly the evidence is mixed. Perhaps some managers are risk-averse. Their salaries are already large so why should they take risks? Or if a firm relies heavily on executive stock option incentives, then perhaps those managers are excessive risk-takers where the risk sometimes pays off and sometimes it does not. In addition, note that it is difficult to relate firm performance to management compensation contracts. If firms perform well, how can we be reliably sure that the incentive-based compensation contract had anything to do with the firm's success?

POTENTIAL "INCENTIVE" PROBLEMS WITH INCENTIVE-BASED COMPENSATION

Problems with Accounting-Based Incentives

The use of accounting profits to measure performance has several potential drawbacks. First, to boost accounting profits, a CEO has an incentive to forego costly research and development that might make the firm more profitable in the future than in the present. Second, accounting profits may be manipulated (see the next chapter). Third, the bonus plan is developed anew each year and, if the threshold cannot be met one year, the CEO has an incentive to move earnings from the present year to the future. This would lower expectations while the next year's bonus plan is being created and artificially increase the executive's chance of receiving that bonus. In short, CEOs may place too much focus on manipulating short-term earnings instead of focusing on long-term earnings and shareholder wealth.

Problems with Stock Option Incentives

There is a good possibility that stock options do not align managerial incentives with shareholder goals. The following list cites potential incentive problems that executive options creates:

1. Shareholder returns combine both stock price appreciation and dividends. The stock option is only affected by price appreciation. Therefore, the CEO might forego increasing dividends in favor of using the cash to try to increase the stock price.
2. The stock price is more likely to increase when the CEO accepts risky projects. Therefore, when a firm uses options to compensate the CEO, she has a tendency to pick a higher risk business strategy.
3. Stock options lose some incentive for the CEO if the stock price falls too far below the strike price. In this case, the options would be too far underwater to motivate the manager effectively.
4. CEOs may try to manipulate earnings and thus maximize profits in one target year to make the stock price more favorable for exercising options. This manipulation can reduce earnings (and consequently the stock price) after the target year. In other words, managers may try to do what they can to time stock price movements to match the time horizons of their stock options.

Another Problem with Executive Stock Options

The very advantage that stock options have of aligning manager incentives with stockholder goals also constitutes a major problem. Stock options are tied to the firm's stock price, which helps align incentives but executives only have partial influence on stock prices. Stock prices are affected by company performance but also by many other factors beyond its control, particularly the strength or weakness of the economy. When the economy thrives, stock prices rise. Even the stock price of a poorly run company may rise, although not as much as its more successful competitors. This occurrence may richly reward executives of poorly run firms through their options when they do not deserve them. Alternatively, the stock market may fall because of poor economic conditions or investor pessimism. A company whose management outperforms its competitors may still find that its stock is falling. In that case, managers should be rewarded but they are not because their options go underwater when the market falls.

Options lose their effectiveness when the stock price falls far below the strike price. The stock price decline could be either related to a company's poor performance or to a general stock market decline. To re-establish motivation for the executives, boards sometimes reprice previously issued options and lower the strike price. Consider the incentives listed above and how they create interesting dynamics for CEO behavior. Executives may choose risky company projects that have a chance of dramatically increasing the stock price. If the projects succeed, the CEO becomes rich and the stockholders experience increased wealth. However, if the projects fail, the stockholders lose money. Meanwhile, the CEO simply asks the board to reprice the options and the CEO can then repeat the strategy. Proponents of option repricing claim that it is necessary to keep executives at the firm. This argument has some truth but that does not change the skewed incentives it causes.

Real-World Examples

Using stock options can be a powerful way to align the interests of managers and shareholders. But is it an effective way? Consider the compensation of Disney CEO Michael Eisner and the value creation at Disney. Eisner was given millions of stock options. If he could add substantial value to Disney, he could cash in for incredible wealth. Consider what he did in the five years starting in 1992. By 1997 Disney was earning three times the profits of 1992. Eisner had added more than $13 billion in value to the firm. The stock price more than doubled from $14.33 to $33.00.[4] Disney's stockholders benefited greatly from this value creation. So did Michael Eisner. His annual salary in 1997 was $750,000 and he received a $9.9 million bonus. He also cashed in $565 million in stock options for a total compensation of $575.7 million.[5]

Unfortunately for Disney shareholders, the story does not end there. Over the next four years after 1997, Disney's profits struggled and the stock price suffered. In 2001, Disney lost $158 million and the stock price ended the year at only $20.72. Eisner received his $1 million salary but he received no bonuses and did not exercise stock options.[6] Eisner's salary and that of other Disney managers has been closely tied to the performance of Disney's profits and stock price. These executives received much lower pay when Disney declined. However, the shareholders lost more than half of the value that was created before 1997. Yet Eisner maintained the incredible income he received for generating that stock price appreciation, even though much of it later disappeared. Most of that income came from Disney stock options.

Examples like that of Eisner and Disney are not fraudulent or illegal. Boards of directors freely give executives stock options and, therefore, create the possibility that only short-term value will be created, not long-term value. However, in other cases managers seem to mislead the public in order to enrich themselves. Consider the management actions at Xerox Corporation.

EXAMPLE 2.2

MANAGEMENT'S BEHAVIOR AT XEROX

In a civil action by the SEC against Xerox, the SEC claimed senior management directed a scheme that improperly accelerated leasing operations revenue from 1997 to 2000. The accounting maneuvering increased revenue by $3 billion and profits by $1.5 billion over that period. In subsequent financial restatements, Xerox shifted out $6.4 billion of revenue for that time. The accounting actions violated generally accepted accounting practices and were not disclosed to shareholders or regulators. Xerox perpetrated the scheme to meet ever increasing internal and analyst earnings expectations and it became common for Xerox executives to assign numerical goals to be produced through accounting gimmickry.[7] Indeed, both the chief financial officer (CFO) and vice chairman of Xerox, and the president of Xerox Europe believed that, excluding accounting maneuvers, the firm had essentially no growth in the 1990s.[8]

The artificial profits helped drive the stock price from a split-adjusted $13 at the end of 1996 to more than $60 in 1999. During this time of inflated stock prices, Xerox CEO Paul Allaire sold stock and profited by $16 million. Xerox executives, in total, sold $79 million worth of stock between 1997 and 1999. Of the total, $48 million was from exercising stock options and the other $31 million was from stock sales. Figure 2.1 shows the relationship between the fraudulent reporting, the stock price, and the executive sales. In April 2002, Xerox admitted to the SEC that it had improperly recorded the earnings and agreed to pay a $10 million fine. Of course, the fine is paid by the firm and thus is a cost to the victimized stockholders.[9] The stock price fell to less than $10 per share, approximately the price 10 years earlier. While the firm has lost any value created in the 1990s, the managers received millions of dollars.

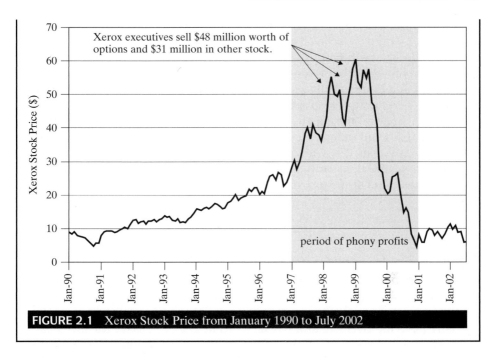

FIGURE 2.1   Xerox Stock Price from January 1990 to July 2002

Expensing Executive Options: An Easy Solution?

Several organizations and people have suggested that the cost of stock options issued to employees and executives should be treated as an expense on the granting firm's financial statements. Even when option exercise prices are at or below current stock prices, they are still valuable. The more stock options granted, and the longer the time allowed to exercise the option, the greater the option value. Using a variation of a formula known as the Black-Scholes option-pricing model, the value of a granted option can be estimated.[10] Under new FASB regulations, effective since June 15, 2005, the value of granted options must now be deducted from the firm's reported income. Some people, like legendary investor Warren Buffett, have been promoting this idea for some time. It appears that there are three reasons that expensing stock options was being promoted.

The first purpose is to have better disclosure and account for the real cost of using options as compensation. The expensing would cause the compensation to be more directly observable to shareholders because it would be reported in the income statements. Also, the expensing would identify that there is a cost to the firm for issuing options. As we discussed earlier, there is a real economic cost (i.e. dilution) to shareholders when executives convert tens, or hundreds, of millions of dollars in options into common stock and then sell it in the stock market. Prior to the push for expensing, this economic cost was not well accounted for on the financial statements of the firm. In other words, this reason for expensing options argues that the economic cost of options should be more transparent.

The second reason for some groups to be proposing option expensing is that it may reduce the amount of options executives receive and thereby reduce their total compensation. The media attention on the tens (or hundreds) of millions of dollars that executives received in the late 1990s brought this topic to more of the public's attention. Without recording the cost of stock options in some way, CEOs are better able to hide their enormous pay. In addition, if the cost of the options is expensed and thereby reduces the firm's reported earnings, then the firm may not be quite so generous in granting them.

The third reason for expensing stock options is the impression that options owned by CEOs and other executives contributed to corporate scandals. That is, options gave executives a mechanism for benefiting from using accounting chicanery to artificially pump up the price of the company stock. If options are not as attractive for firms to issue, then maybe there will be less of an incentive for executives to time the market.

However, the expensing of options might not represent an easy and automatic solution to the problems inherent in executive stock options. Some industries, like technology, use options as compensation for many employees, not just executives. For example, Microsoft issues options to most of its employees. Indeed, many technology firms are adamantly opposed to the new FASB regulation.[11] Even some non-tech companies use options to pay middle and lower managers, like Kohls Corp, a department store chain. Also it is common for start-up companies to partially pay employees in stock options to help compensate for low salaries. Using this type of pay system, the young company can conserve one of its most precious resources, cash, and motivate employees to work hard. What happens to these compensation systems if options are expensed? The reduction in reported earnings may cause the companies to curtail option programs. This could inhibit the growth of new companies. It could even have an impact on the economy since new companies are an important source of new jobs.

OTHER COMPENSATION

Executives often receive other forms of compensation that are sometimes not reported to the SEC on official documents. The old style perk of a company paying for a CEO's club membership may come to mind but that is passé compared to modern perks. The company will frequently pay for financial advisors, luxury cars and chauffeurs, personal travel, Manhattan apartments, and more.

Retirement (or resignation) compensation is also popular. For example, when former CEO and current chairman of FleetBoston, Terrence Murray retires, he will receive a pension payment of $5.8 million per year. In addition, he can use corporate jets for his travel (and that of his guests) for up to 150 hours per year.[12] Louis Gerstner retired as CEO of IBM (though he continued for a time as chairman) in March 2002. In addition to his $2 million yearly pension, he has access to corporate jets, cars, and apartments for 20 years. If IBM wants Gerstner's advice, he will be paid $600 per hour.[13]

Another benefit is obtaining a company loan. Executives commonly borrow hundreds of thousands, or even millions of dollars at extremely low interest rates — sometimes even interest free. These loans may be used to purchase expensive homes: Wells Fargo CEO Richard Kovacevich borrowed $1 million for a house down payment. The savings on low interest loans can quickly add up to tens or hundreds of thousands of dollars. Frequently, executives do not even pay back the loans. Mattel Corp. absolved ousted CEO Jill Barad from repaying a $7.2 million loan and then paid her an additional $3.3 million to cover the cost of resulting additional taxes.[14] The new CEO, Robert Eckert, received a $5.5 million loan and will not have to repay it if he stays with the firm for two years. A similar arrangement exists with Compaq Chairman and CEO Michael Capellas for his $5 million loan.

CRIME AND PUNISHMENT

Earlier, we stated that managers will work hard on behalf of shareholders if they are carefully monitored and if they have the right incentives. Most of this book discusses monitoring. This chapter has discussed managerial incentives. However, perhaps a third way to align the incentives of mangers with shareholders is to increase the penalty for mangers who intentionally and knowingly mislead and behave in ways that are not beneficial to shareholders.

Under the new Sarbanes-Oxley Act, the firm's executives now have to sign off certifying the appropriateness of the financial statements. In addition, the Act increased the scope and penalties for white-collar crimes. In July 2005, Bernie Ebbers, founder and former chief executive of WorldCom, was sentenced to 25 years in prison for his involvement in WorldCom's $11 billion accounting fraud. At the time of this writing, Dennis Kozlowski, former CEO of Tyco, is awaiting sentencing following his guilty verdict of grand larceny against Tyco. Will punishment serve to deter managerial misbehavior? Time will tell. But it is often the case that "carrots" or rewards are better motivators than "sticks" or punishment.

INTERNATIONAL PERSPECTIVE – CEO COMPENSATION AROUND THE WORLD

Paying the top officer in the company with long-term incentive awards is most common in the U.S. Figure 2.2 shows the compensation of CEOs around the world, split into three categories. These categories are fixed pay (base salary and benefits), variable pay (incentive-type instruments like stock options), and perquisites. The data comes from surveys conducted by Towers Perrin.[15] The figure shows that 63 percent, on average, of a U.S. CEO's pay is variable in nature.

The variable component of CEO pay is much higher in the U.S. than most other countries. Only Singapore (59 percent) and Canada (52 percent) have similar fractions of variable pay. In contrast, CEOs from many countries earn most of their compensation from fixed pay. For example, for CEOs in China (except Hong Kong) 79 percent of their compensation is fixed. The percentages for Sweden and Belgium are 78 percent and 73 percent, respectively. Variable pay is at least 50 percent of total compensation for only 5 of the 23 countries. India, one of the five countries with less than 50 percent composition in fixed pay, pays

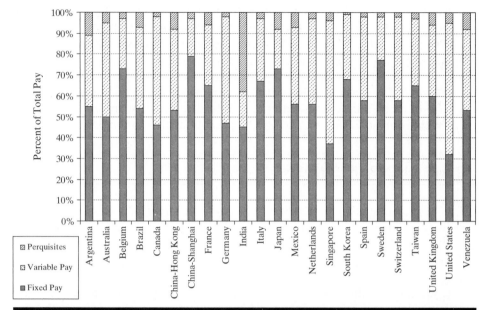

FIGURE 2.2   Components of CEO Compensation around the World, 2003

an extraordinary 38 percent of total compensation in perquisites. From these statistics it is clear that there is a large variation in how top execitives are paid throughout the world.

Summary

A major disadvantage of the public ownership form of the corporation is the separation of ownership and control. Managers who control the firm are supposed to act in the firms' shareholders' best interests but they may be tempted to take advantage of their control power to satisfy their own needs and desires, often to the deriment of the stockholders. To inhibit poor managerial behavior, shareholders try to align the executive's interests with their own through incentive programs involving stocks and stock options. Many people believe that stock and option incentives reduce this conflict between those who own the firm and those who control it. When executives work hard to increase the firm's stock price over the long term, both the shareholders and the executives reap the benefit.

However, whether or not the incentives work results in much debate. For example, stock options create an economic cost to the firm and sometimes do not create the correct rewards for good and poor managers. In addition, stock options also create other incentives that are not aligned with stockholder interests.

At the beginning of this chapter, we cited examples of managerial temptations. We also said that if managers have the right incentives, then we may be able to contol these temptations. However, note that these incentives or "rewards" potentially creates yet another managerial temptation—the temptation to commit fraud to reap these rewards. For example, incentive-based compensation tied to reported earnings or stock prices create the temptation for managers to manipulate or even falsify earnings. If incentive compensation is imperfect, then monitors are needed. The rest of this book describes and discusses those monitors.

WEB Info about Executive Compensation

Towers Perrin
www.towersperrin.com

AFL-CIO Corporate Watch
www.aflcio.org/corporatewatch/

Mercer Human Resource Consulting
www.mercerhr.com

Review Questions

1. In what ways can managers harm stockholders?
2. What is the rationale behind firms using executive stock options?
3. What potential misalignments do stock options create?
4. When might options fail to reward good managers?
5. List the pros and cons of compensating a CEO with stock options.
6. How does the repricing of stock options affect a manager's incentives?
7. How does executive pay in the U.S. compare to pay internationally?

Discussion Questions

1. How would you design an executive compensation contract to ensure managers have the right incentives? Do you think managers will like it?
2. Do you think executive options should be expensed? Why or why not?
3. What do you think CEO compensation will be like in the near future? Maybe it will be more conservative, but then do you think this will help or harm the future growth of corporate America? Discuss the cost-benefit trade-offs.
4. Do you think firms should force executives to own the firm's stock? This might create a near-perfect alignment between managers and shareholders, but do not forget that executives already have their entire peronal wealth (i.e. their salaries) staked to the firm.

Exercises

1. KPMG was the auditing firm for Xerox during the time it was accused of manipulating its accounting figures (see the Xerox example). To what degree is KPMG to blame for fraud? Like Xerox, should it be held accountable? What has the SEC done about KPMG's role?
2. The former CEO of Tyco, Dennis Kozlowski, has been accused of many abuses of the stockholders' money; describe some of these. John, Tim, and Michael Rigas were arrested for perpetrating massive financial fraud and looting Adelphia Communications. Describe what happened.
3. Obtain the total compensation of five CEOs of companies (of different sizes and in different industries). Compare and contrast their compensation and comment on the potential alignment or misalignment of incentives.

4. For the five CEOs you researched for Exercise #3 above, try to argue that they deserved their pay. Then try to argue that they did not deserve their pay.

5. Try to find a real-world U.S. example of what you think is a fair executive option. Describe the details of the option and explain why you think it is fair.

Exercises for Non-U.S. Students

1. Does your country use executive stock options? If so, do some research and describe its experience with them. If not, then do you think it should? Why or why not? Is there anything unique about your country that makes executive options more or less attractive than in the U.S.?

2. What are the primary ways in which CEOs are rewarded in your country?

Do you think they are effective? Why or why not?

3. Obtain the total compensation of five CEOs of companies in your country (of different sizes and in different industries). First, try to argue that they each deserved their pay. Then try to argue that they each did not deserve their pay.

Endnotes

1. Much of the compensation description in this section is summaries from Kevin Murphy, "Executive Compensation," in *Handbook of Labor Economics*, ed. O. Ashenfelter and D. Card, Vol. 3B. Amsterdam: North-Hollan Publishers, 1999.

2. The Wall Street Journal/Mercer Human Resource Consulting, "2004 CEO Compensation Survey and Trends," May 2005.

3. Michael Jensen and Kevin Murpher, "Performance Pay and Top Management Incentives," Journal of Political Economy 98 (1990): 225–263.

4. These are split-adjusted stock price figures.

5. Tim Smart, "An Eye-Popping Year for Executive Pay," *Washington Post*, March 22, 1998, H1.

6. Richard Verrier, "Eisner's Paycheck Humbled in 2001," *Los Angeles Times*, January 5, 2002, C1.

7. James Bandler and Mark Maremont, "Seeing Red: How Ex-Accountant Added Up to Trouble for Humbled Xerox," *Wall Street Journal*, June 28, 2001, A1.

8. SEC v. Xerox Corporation, Civil Action No. 02-272789, Southern District of New York, U.S. District Court, (April 11, 2002).

9. Andrew Countryman, "Focus of Xerox Probe Shifts to Stock Sales," *Chicago Tribune*, July 2, 2002, 1.

10. *http://en.wikipedia.org/wiki/Stock_options#Valuation*.

11. *http://news.com.com/Businesses+rally+against+stock+option+plan/2100–1022_3–5169448.html?tag=nl*.

12. Joann Lublin, "As CEOs' Reported Salaries and Bonuses Get Pinched, Many Chiefs Are Finding Hidden Ways to Increase Their Compensation," *Wall Street Journal*, April 11, 2002, B7.

13. Joann Lublin, "How CEOs Retire in Style," *Wall Street Journal*, September 13, 2002, B1.

14. Gary Strauss, "Many Execs Pocket Perks Aplenty," *USA Today*, May 1, 2001, B1.

15. Specifically, the data are from 2003–2004 Worldwide Total Remuneration study by Towers Perrin.

3

ACCOUNTANTS AND AUDITORS

A ccountants and auditors are an important part of any corporate monitoring system. Accountants keep track of the quantitative financial information of the firm. Because mistakes and other problems (such as intentional fraud) may occur with accounting, there are auditors that review the financial information. As such, auditors may be in the best position to monitor companies. In this process, auditors obtain private information about the company that others cannot obtain, and they use this information to determine whether the company's public financial statements reflect the true level of business being conducted. Banks, creditors, and others rely on these statements to get an accurate picture of the firm's business activities and financial health. Investors use these public statements to assess the value of the company. Therefore, the auditor's candid evaluation of those statements is crucial. This chapter first provides an overview of accounting and auditing. Then it discusses how accountants and auditors might contribute to financial fraud and how they might expose fraud.

ACCOUNTING FUNCTIONS

Historically, accounting has been the function of gathering, compiling, reporting, and archiving a firm's business activities. This accounting information helps individuals in many roles who depend on it to make decisions. For convenience, those who need accounting information are categorized as either insiders or outsiders of the firm.

Accounting for Inside Use

Management accounting is the development of information for insiders, such as company managers. Managers use this information to measure the progress toward their goals and highlight any potential problems in advance. For example, managers want to know which products have the best sales and which are selling poorly. Which products tend to sell together? How is inventory being managed? What about cash? Will the firm have enough cash to pay its upcoming debt payments?

Accountants answer these questions with budgets, variance reports, sensitivity analysis, revenue reports, cost projections, and even analysis of competitors. When firms consider how to expand products and services, managerial accountants help formulate profit projections from revenue and cost projections. In short, managerial accounting has historically played a large part in the control and evaluation of the business and its performance.

Accounting for Outside Use

Outsiders of the firm also use accounting information. Investors, banks, the government, and other stakeholders have a keen interest in the financial health of the firm. Banks and other creditors want to know if the firm will be able to pay its debts. Shareholders want to know how profitable the firm is and how profitable it may be in the future. Employees might have a double interest because they have their careers and employment at stake and they might be investors through their retirement plans as well.

Financial accounting provides information for outsiders. Whereas managerial accounting reports may break down performance for managers by individual products or regions of the country, financial reports summarize the business as a whole, although they can be broken into business segments and regions. In the case of publicly held companies, these reports are the quarterly and annual financial statements that they must file with the Securities and Exchange Commission (SEC).

The three main **financial statements** (income statement, balance sheet, and statement of cash flows) and other pieces of important information (e.g. popular press articles and analyst recommendations) are used by outsiders to determine the firm's value, profits, and its risk. Outsiders want to be able to compare firms easily. Thus the SEC requires that these accounting statements adhere to a uniform set of standards known as generally accepted accounting principles (GAAP) for public companies. These statements are prepared by the accountants of the firm and reviewed by independent accountants from an auditing firm (more on auditors later in the chapter).

The Internal Revenue Service (IRS) also requires accounting information for tax purposes. The accountants of the firm report profits or losses to the IRS and determine the tax liability. Interestingly, accounting methods and business record-keeping can be very different for reports to managers, for public financial statements and for the IRS. For example, there are ambiguities regarding how to record some transactions in GAAP. When reporting business activities in an annual report, choices are made that maximize earnings in order to make them appear stronger than they would otherwise be, in the hope of driving up the firm's stock price. When IRS forms are being completed, choices are made to minimize earnings in order to minimize tax expenditures.[1]

PROBLEMS THAT MAY OCCUR IN ACCOUNTING

As with any kind of record-keeping there are potential problems. First, unintentional errors are possible. Sometimes these errors are due to miscaluations or due to applying an expense to the wrong accounting ledger. Another potential problem occurs when judgements are required. Should firms count all receivables when they know that some clients and customers might never pay for goods or services rendered? Finally, accountants could perpetuate fraud. For example, they could overstate income, understate liabilities, or overstate assets such as receiveables. Or they could be tricked by a manager to inadvertently commit fraud on his behalf. Accounting fraud is probably the largest potential problem with accounting, as it is intentional (either by a manager or by an accountant) and hurts the firm's stakeholders, including its shareholders. Because of these potential accounting problems, the role of auditors is important, which we discuss next.

AUDITING

Internal Auditors

Many firms have **internal auditors**. Their responsibility is to oversee the firm's financial and operating procedures, to check the accuracy of the financial record-keeping, to implement improvements with internal control, to ensure compliance with accounting regulations, and to detect fraud. Firms are not required to have internal auditors but many firms have them to enhance their accounting and internal control efficiency. In fact, the people who initially detected financial fraud at WorldCom were the company's own internal auditors.

EXAMPLE 3.1

EXERPTED STORY FROM THE *WALL STREET JOURNAL*[2]

Sitting in his cubicle at WorldCom Inc. headquarters one afternoon in May, Gene Morse stared at an accounting entry for $500 million in computer expenses. He could not find any invoices or documentation to back up the stunning number.

"Oh my God," he muttered to himself. The auditor immediately took his discovery to his boss, Cynthia Cooper, the company's vice president of internal audit . . .

By June 23, they had unearthed $3.8 billion in misallocated expenses and phony accounting entries. It all added up to an accounting fraud, acknowledged by the company, which turned out to be the largest in corporate history. Their discoveries sent WorldCom into bankruptcy, left thousands of their colleagues without jobs, and roiled the stock market.

Behind the tale of accounting chicanery lies the untold detective story of three young internal auditors . . . Ms. Cooper, 38 years old, headed a department of 24 auditors and support staffers, many of whom viewed her as quiet but strong willed . . . Mr. Morse, 41, was known for his ability to use technology to ferret out information . . . The third member of the team was Glyn Smith, 34, a senior manager under Ms. Cooper.

External Auditors

External auditors are accountants from outside the firm, who review the firm's financial statements and its procedures for producing them. Their job is to attest to the fairness of the statements and that they materially represent the condition of the firm. Often the external auditor will assess the system and procedures used by internal auditors to see if they can rely on the internally-generated reports when conducting their own audit.[3] To conduct their external audit, the auditors might:

1. conduct interviews with the firm's employees to assess the quality of the internal audit system;
2. make their own observations of the firm's assets such as inventory levels;
3. check sample balance-sheet transactions;
4. confirm with the firm's customers and clients to check the accuracy of short-term assets and liabilities; and
5. conduct their own financial statements analysis such as comparing the firm's financial ratios from one period to the next.

Once they have completed their audit, they will generate a report (see General Motor's example below).

Because external auditors are supposed to be independent of the firm being audited and because their explicit job is to check for financial mis-statements and adherence to GAAP, it is they who must ensure the accuracy of the firm's financial information for shareholders. Today, the four largest accounting firms, known as the "Big Four," that provide external audits, are PriceWaterhouseCoopers, Deloitte & Touche, Ernst & Young, and KPMG.

EXAMPLE 3.2

INDEPENDENT AUDITORS REPORT FOR GENERAL MOTORS[4]

General Motors Corporation, its Directors, and Stockholders:

We have audited the accompanying Consolidated Balance Sheets of General Motors Corporation and subsidiaries (the Corporation) as of December 31, 2004 and 2003, and the related Consolidated Statements of Income, Cash Flows, and Stockholders' Equity for each of the three years in the period ended December 31, 2004. Our audits also included the Supplemental Information to the Consolidated Balance Sheets and Consolidated Statements of Income and Cash Flows (the financial statement schedules). These financial statements and financial statement schedules are the responsibility of the Corporation's management. Our responsibility is to express an opinion on these financial statements and financial statement schedules based on our audits.

We conducted our audits in accordance with the standards of the Public Company Accounting Oversight Board (United States). Those standards require that we plan and perform the audit to obtain reasonable assurance about whether the financial statements are free of material mis-statement. An audit includes examining, on a test basis, evidence supporting the amounts and disclosures in the financial statements. An audit also includes assessing the accounting principles used and significant estimates made by management, as well as evaluating the overall financial statement presentation. We believe that our audits provide a reasonable basis for our opinion.

In our opinion, such consolidated financial statements present fairly, in all material respects, the financial position of General Motors Corporation and subsidiaries at December 31, 2004 and 2003, and the results of their operations and their cash flows for each of the three years in the period ended December 31, 2004, in conformity with accounting principles generally accepted in the United States of America. Also, in our opinion, such financial statement schedules, when considered in relation to the basic consolidated financial statements taken as a whole, present fairly, in all material respects, the information set forth therein.

Deloitte & Touche LLP
Detroit, Michigan
March 14, 2005

As discussed in Note 1 to the consolidated financial statements, the Corporation:

1. effective from July 1, 2003, began consolidating certain variable interest entities to conform to FASB Interpretation No. 46, *Consolidation of Variable Interest Entities;* and

2. effective from January 1, 2003, began expensing the fair market value of newly granted stock options and other stock-based compensation awards issued to employees to conform to Statement of Financial Accounting Standards No. 123, *Accounting for Stock-Based Compensation.*

We have also audited, in accordance with the standards of the Public Company Accounting Oversight Board (United States), the effectiveness of the Corporation's internal control over financial reporting as of December 31, 2004, based on the criteria established in *Internal Control – Integrated Framework* issued by the Committee of Sponsoring Organizations of the Treadway Commission and our report dated March 14, 2005 expressed an unqualified opinion on management's assessment of the effectiveness of the Corporation's internal control over financial reporting and an unqualified opinion on the effectiveness of the Corporation's internal control over financial reporting.

How the Nature of External Auditing has Evolved Since the Late 1930s

While banks and other creditors have always wanted independent verification of a firm's financial health, the role of monitoring a firm's financial statements was cemented by the Securities Act of 1933 and the Securities Exchange Act of 1934. During the Great Depression, after the corporate spending excesses of the late 1920s, the country was reeling from business scandals. Congress reacted with legislation that called for stronger oversight and regulation and required annual independent audits of all public companies.

Because of this legislative requirement, in the late 1930s and 1940s accounting firms flourished with the increased demand for auditing services. Initially the high demand resulted from the new laws that required independent verification of a firm's financial books. The demand for auditing services continued to grow as the economy eventually picked up and the number of public firms increased. There was plenty of business for auditing firms and the environment was such that they could play an effective role as independent monitors—even becoming adversarial with the firm if necessary.

In the 1970s and 1980s, however, the auditing business began to change. The number of new companies that needed auditing services was no longer expanding. If auditing firms wanted to grow, they had to steal clients away from other auditing firms. The code of ethics was changed to permit advertising and other competitive practices. Auditing firms began to advertise and cut their prices to lure new clients. The relationship between the auditing firm and the audited company also began to change; with other audit firms courting them and corporate managers no longer tolerating adversarial auditors. Auditors became friendlier in order to keep their clients, especially the larger companies. Because of the prestige associated with having Fortune 500 companies as clients, auditing firms became less confrontational in order to keep them as clients. During this period, auditing firms also developed consulting services to advise companies on how to improve their accounting methods and business activities. This provided both another source of income for accounting firms and a way to solidify their relationships with company management.

ACCOUNTING OVERSIGHT

Accountants are responsible for the firm's financial information and auditors are supposed to monitor and check the financial information for accuracy. However, both accountants and auditors are governed by regulations and regulatory bodies. The **Financial Accounting Standards Board (FASB)**, a non-government entity made up of members of the accounting, business, and academic professions, sets accounting standards known as **Generally Accepted Accounting Principles (GAAP)**. The SEC recognizes FASB as authoritative, which means that the SEC recognizes FASB decisions on creating and amending GAAP, though the SEC and the U.S. Congress have been known to influence FASB accounting policies.

Associations in the accounting profession sponsor FASB and, to promote independence, its seven board members are required to serve full time and divest their interests in their former employers. Even non-CPAs serve on the FASB board.

External auditors are required by the SEC to make sure the financial statements adhere to GAAP. An organization called the **American Institute of Certified Public Accontants (AICPA)** had set auditing standards and had governed external audits. However, with the passage of the 2002 Sarbanes-Oxley Act, a new board called the **Public Company Accounting Oversight Board (PCAOB)** was established that would, in effect, replace AICPA's role as the regulatory body overseeing the auditing profession. Under the 2002 Act, all public firms have to be registered with PCAOB and meet its standards. The PCAOB also oversees public accounting firms. The example of General Motors' audit report indicates that the auditor conducted its report in accordance to PCAOB standards. In Chapter 9, we discuss the relationship between the SEC and the accounting profession and in Chapter 10 we discuss the new 2002 Act.

While the PCAOB now sets auditing standards, the AICPA still remains an active organization. It is the largest association for CPAs, with over 330,000 regular members. In order to promote a high ethical standard for association members, the AICPA maintains and distributes the AICPA Professional Code of Conduct. The Code provides Principles and Rules that govern the professional behavior of members.

THE CHANGING ROLE OF ACCOUNTING – MANAGING EARNINGS

During the last two decades, the role of accounting departments within companies has changed. Instead of simply providing information to insiders and outsiders, accounting departments have begun the transition into being profit centers. Instead of simply reporting the quarterly profits of the firm, accounting departments are asked to increase profits through application of accounting methods. In some areas, the ambiguity in GAAP and the subjectivity of business activities provide for different ways of accounting for the same transaction. Different methods often lead to different levels of reportable profits. The reporting of profits, therefore, can be both an art and a science. This process is known as **managing earnings**.

For example, accountants may feel pressure to **meet internal targets**. Managers may want to show their employees and the board of directors that they were able to increase revenue and decrease costs. As discussed in the prior chapter, when firms meet internally set targets, such as target ROAs or ROEs, it may lead to a raise or a bonus for the CEO and other managers.

Accountants may also feel pressure to **meet external targets**. Analysts make predictions about firms' profitability measured by earnings per share (EPS). If the firm fails to meet these expectations, then the share price will decline. Therefore, accountants must use whatever methods possible to meet these external expectations. In addition, accountants may be asked to **window dress** the firm's financial statements to improve its chances of getting a favorable external financing arrangement, such as a low interest loan. Accountants could stretch assumptions to increase reported income or reduce existing liabilities.

Another example of variations in accounting method applications relates to the desire of companies to exhibit a steady growth in profits, that is, to **smooth income**. If the profits generated by business activities grow, but at an erratic pace, then accountants are asked to smooth out the earnings over time. Smooth earnings give shareholders a sense of reduced risk. Accountants can defer or accelerate the recognition of some revenues to smooth reported income from year to year.

EXAMPLE 3.3

GENERAL ELECTRIC'S SMOOTH EARNINGS

General Electric (GE) has been accused of using accounting manipulations to manage its earnings.[5] Notice in Figure 3.1 how steady the growth in GE's earnings has been, especially since 1995. The accusations claim that GE employs a number of confusing but apparently legal gimmicks to achieve its consistent growth. For example, GE's financing division, GE Capital, can reduce current earnings for the firm by being pessimistic in its estimates of losses from problem loans. If those loans eventually are repaid, future profits will increase. The maneuver effectively shifts some earnings into the future. If the firm is in need of more earnings in the present, it can conduct a real estate sale and leaseback. The transaction could work like this. GE sells a factory to investors for $100 million. GE signs a long-term lease with the investors so that GE still uses the factory. However, because the factory has been depreciated to $50 million, GE can claim the difference as a capital gain and increase pretax profits by $50 million. Alternatively the profit could be amortized over the life of the lease. Due to GAAP ambiguities and loopholes, firms can choose the methods that benefit them the most.

Both taking reserves for bad loans and the real estate sale/leaseback are perfectly legal. However, their accounting treatment assumes that these transactions occur as normal business activities but some firms use them as accounting devices to manage earnings over time. Other firms can be used as examples for managing earnings. For instance, IBM has also been accused of taking financial steps in the 1990s to create double-digit earnings growth when revenue grew at only 5 percent.[6] However, GE holds a special place in the investment industry because it is the only company in the Dow Jones Industrial Average that was an original Dow Jones firm when the index was created more than 100 years ago.

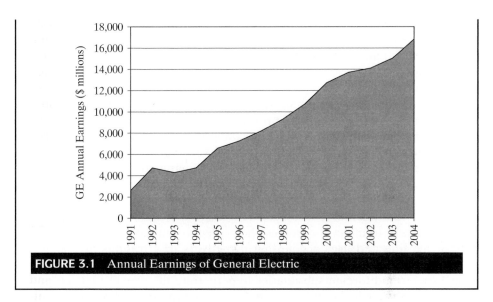

FIGURE 3.1 Annual Earnings of General Electric

FROM MANIPULATION TO FRAUD

The accounting schemes that companies use can be either simple or complex. Indeed, modern accounting and auditing firms recommend structuring deals in a way that may not have any value in conducting business, but the deals spin off either profits or losses that can be reversed in the future to manage earnings. A question often asked is how much can companies manipulate accounting figures before they cross the line into fraud? Where is the line?

For example, a firm could sell an asset, such as a truck, to its own subsidiary (e.g. technically a special-purpose entity created as an off-shore partnership) for an outrageously high price. The book value of the truck is low. Therefore the firm books a large capital gain and profits go up. The subsidiary capitalizes the cost of the truck, which means that the subsidiary will have to report lower earnings in each of the future years in which the truck cost is depreciated. In effect, the firm takes a profit now that it will have to offset as expenses in the future related to the sale of a truck it still owns! While these types of maneuvers help to manage earnings, their effect is limited unless the company crosses the line and uses them fraudulently.

The pressure on accounting departments to smooth earnings, or even produce earnings can be intense when the firm is not meeting investor (analyst) expectations. Because the role of accounting has changed and accounting departments are viewed as profit centers, they are pressed to make up shortfalls created by the business operations of the firm. Sometimes firms and their accountants and auditors cross way over the line to fraudulent practices. Recent examples of alleged accounting fraud are WorldCom, Enron, Rite Aid, Adelphia, and Tyco. For example, on June 25, 2002, WorldCom disclosed that roughly $3.8 billion had been improperly booked as capital investments instead of operating expenses over the previous five quarters. Specifically, WorldCom had to pay fees to other phone companies in order for them to transfer WorldCom customers' calls immediately.[7] By capitalizing these fees, contrary to GAAP, WorldCom pushed current expenses into the future, thereby boosting current earnings (at the expense of future earnings).

Enron used sophisticated and complicated methods to generate inflated reported earnings. For example, Enron would sell assets to its own subsidiaries for high prices to book huge capital gains and profits. Enron would also enter into contracts to sell energy to a customer for 30 years. Then they underestimated the cost of providing that energy, thereby overestimating the annual profit of the contract.[8] Enron would also book all thirty years of these inflated profits in the current year. This made Enron appear incredibly profitable over the short-term but was detrimental to its longer-term financial health. While these types of maneuvers help to manage earnings, their affect is limited unless the company crosses the line and uses accounting maneuvers in a fraudulent manner. It appears that Enron did go over that line. Enron created complex partnership arrangements and foreign subsidiaries to perpetrate the worst of its accounting offenses. For its role in Enron's questionable accounting and subsequent obstruction of justice, Arthur Anderson, previously the fifth largest public accounting firm, relinquished its license to conduct audits.

So while managing earnings can be legal, there is a fine line between legal accounting maneuvering and accounting fraud. It is important to point out, however, that when accounting fraud does occur, accountants and auditors can claim that they were fooled by management. However, while accountants and auditors might not be engaged in fraudulent acts, it does not entirely absolve them from responsibility. A part of their job is to detect incorrect accounting numbers, whether they are a result of a mistake or a fraudulent act.

EXAMPLE 3.4

RITE AID'S OVERSTATEMENT OF INCOME

On June 21, 2002, a federal grand jury indicted four former and current executives of Rite Aid for conducting a wide-ranging scheme to overstate income.[9] The SEC noted in its investigation of the matter that Rite Aid reported false and misleading information in 10 different areas, ranging from reducing its costs and accelerating revenue to manipulating numbers between quarterly and annual reports.[10] Indeed, Rite Aid restated earnings for its fiscal year 1998 in a way that caused $305 million in net income to become $186 million in net losses. The restatement in fiscal year 1999 was from a $143 million profit to a $422.5 million loss, and a total of more than $1 billion in earnings disappeared.

Figure 3.2 shows the price of Rite Aid's stock during this period and its relationship to stated and restated earnings. Rite Aid stated that it earned $116.7 million in fiscal year 1997, which ended February 28, 1998. The stock price at this time was $21 per share. As indicated above, Rite Aid then stated earnings of $305 million in 1998 and the stock price rose to $34.25. The stock price reached its maximum of $50.94 on January 8, 1999. A few months later the firm reported fiscal year 1999 earnings of $143 million. However, investors started to realize that something was wrong. By July 10, 2000, the stock had slowly fallen to $7.85 per share. The stock price fell to $5 per share the next day when Rite Aid restated its earnings for 1998 to 2000. The stock spent the summer of 2002 at less than $2.50 per share.

Rite Aid's stock price was artificially inflated in the late 1990s because of fraud in financial reporting. The investors who purchased Rite Aid stock in 1999 did so based on false information, thinking the firm profitable and growing. As a result they lost money. Existing investors should also have been informed about the extent of the firm's losses so that they could decide whether to keep or sell their stock. After the truth finally became public, it was too late—shareholders had lost most of their investments.

FIGURE 3.2   Rite Aid Earnings and Associated Stock Price

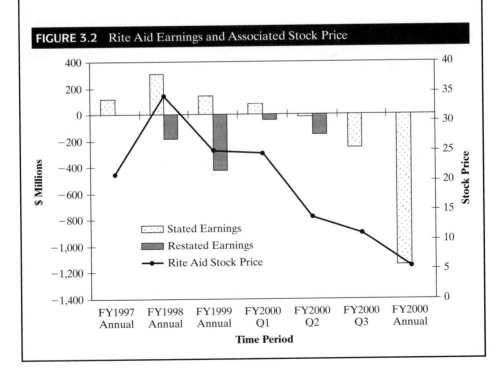

AUDITORS AS CONSULTANTS

Business consulting firms typically advise firms on tactical issues, such as how to enter a new market, and strategic issues, such as acquiring or spinning off other firms. When it comes to consulting, the leading firm is McKinsey & Company, which advises more than half of the Fortune 500 firms. In 2001, McKinsey had 7,700 consultants in 84 locations worldwide and generated $3.4 billion in revenue.[11] This represents a more than 40 percent market share of the consulting business. Accounting firms want to gain some of this business.

One potential problem for a firm's shareholders occurs when a consulting firm also conducts auditing services for the company. The income for conducting an audit is far lower than the fees earned for consulting. Therefore auditors may be pressured by their own accounting firm to overlook borderline practices, especially when consultants advocate those practices. This situation represents a serious conflict of interest for the auditors. Their responsibility should be effective monitoring for the shareholders but instead their inclination may be different because their bonuses often depend on how much money the consulting group earns for the accounting firm.

The Public Company Accounting Reform and Investor Protection Act of 2002, which is intended to separate auditors and consultants, prohibits accounting firms from providing both auditing and consulting activities to the same company. Chapter 10 of this book discusses the Act in more detail.

EXAMPLE 3.5

TYCO'S TAX SAVING STRATEGY

Consultants commonly advise companies on tax reduction strategies. Consider the efforts that Tyco International Ltd. makes to reduce its U.S. taxes. Tyco, an electrical manufacturing and services firm, moved to the tax haven of Bermuda in 1996.[12] The company has also created more than 150 subsidiaries in other tax-friendly places, such as Barbados and the Cayman Islands. The purpose of these entities is not, for the most part, to conduct business, but to shelter income from the U.S. and to avoid taxes. Tyco claims that these strategies cut its 2001 tax bill by $600 million and Tyco pays the most taxes to countries other than the U.S. All this happens beyond the eyes of the shareholder. The annual report does not provide information about its mysterious subsidiaries, which have names like Driftwood, Bunga Bevaru, and Silver Avenue Holdings.

INTERNATIONAL PERSPECTIVE

Compared to the accounting systems used internationally, the system in the U.S. is quite rigorous. Characteristics of a high-quality system are many shareholder rights and strong protection of those rights. This protection comes from strong laws that are enforced and accounting standards that are unambiguous.

In a recent study of 31 countries, the U.S. was found to have the best legal environment to discourage earnings manipulations and smoothing.[13] Australia, Ireland, Canada, and the U.K. also have good investor protection and enforcement histories. Countries where earnings manipulations are more common include Austria, Italy, Germany, South Korea, and Taiwan. While some shareholders might question the quality of the financial statements in the U.S., the accounting numbers of some firms that are not based in the U.S. could be of much lower quality. The scandals in some U.S. firms parallel some recent international scandals (see Parmalat example below).

The **International Accounting Standards Board (IASB)** is developing a single set of high-quality, understandable, and enforceable global accounting standards that require transparent and comparable information in general-purpose financial statements. In addition, IASB wants to encourage convergence in accounting standards of individual countries around the world. Whether the SEC will accept financial statements using these international standards rather than U.S. GAAP, remains to be seen.

EXAMPLE 3.6

PARMALAT'S ACCOUNTING SCANDAL

Apparently U.S. firms do not have a monoply on ficticious revenue. On the heels of the Enron and Tyco scandals, a non-U.S. industry giant also experienced its own shocking accounting scandal. The eighth largest industrial firm in Italy, Parmalat, is perhaps best known in the U.S. for its pasteurized Parmalat milk, Archway cookies, and Black Diamond cheeses. The firm was exposed for a $10 billion accounting fraud. One of Parmalat's fraudulent accounting practices involved the setting up of numerous shell companies to generate fake profits. Parmalat's external auditor, up-and-coming firm Grant Thornton, might have assisted Parmalat with some of its accounting fraud. Under Italian law, a firm must change its external auditor every nine years. So when Grant Thornton's time was up, it suggested to Parmalat to spin off several of its businesses so that it could continue to keep various Parmalat concerns as clients. These spun-off subsidiaries made fake payments to Parmalat in the form of owed debt. Meanwhile, these

(Continued)

(*Continued*)

subsidiaries created false accounts to make it look like they could pay the debt. However, not all of Parmalat's frauds were this complicated. Parmalat executives forged a document using Bank of America letterhead to claim that Parmalat had a $5 billion bank deposit. They ran this document through the fax machine a few times to make it look "authentic." Parmalat was declared bankrupt in 2003. Carlisto Tanzi, the founder of Parmalat, and his son and daughter, along with several other former Parmalat executives, were arrested for financial fraud.

Sources: www.wsws.org/articles/2004/jan2004/parm-j06.shtml
http://en.wikipedia.org/wiki/parmalat

Summary

Accountants keep track of the firm's financial records. Internal and external auditors review these records. Therefore auditors are an important part of the governance system. However, the role of accounting has changed in recent years. Aside from keeping financial records, they are asked to manage earnings to meet internal and external targets, to window dress the firm's financial statements, and to smooth reported income from year to year. Sometimes when accountants "work the numbers," they are treading a danerous line between manipulating figures within the rules and outright fraud. Auditors might be fooled by the accounting tricks, which weakens their ability to detect errors. Further, auditors might even be tempted to participate in this dangerous treading. They want clients to be happy and they are subject to a possible conflict of interest problem if they are also the firm's consultants. With the passage of the new Sarbanes-Oxley Act, auditors are no longer allowed to provide consulting services to the firms they are auditing and a new regulatory body has been created to oversee independent audits. Even before the passage of the Act, the U.S. probably had, and probably still has, the best accounting and auditing system and standards in the world.

WEB Info about Accounting and Auditing

Institute of Internal Auditors
www.theiia.org/

Public Company Accounting Oversight Board
www.pcaobus.org

American Institute of Certified Public Accountants
www.aicpa.org

International Accounting Standards Board
www.iasb.org

Review Questions

1. What is the role of management accounting, financial accounting, internal auditing, and external auditing?
2. What has weakened the ability of external auditors to conduct objective audits?
3. Who regulates accounting and auditing?
4. What is meant by "managing earnings?"
5. Give examples of how firms can manipulate earnings. Give examples of how firms commit accounting fraud.

Discussion Questions

1. Smoothing accounting earnings, from year to year, could make the stock price less volatile (i.e. less risky). So is smoothing, or managing, earnings good or bad for shareholders? Compare and contrast the advantages versus disadvantages of smoothing earnings.
2. How would you improve the system of external auditing in the U.S.? Make sure you weigh the costs and benefits to your ideas. Also make sure you describe how your ideas are feasible.
3. Do you think the U.S. should adopt the International Accounting Standards that IASB has created? Do you think the rest of the world should adopt U.S. GAAP? For the latter question, first argue "no" and then argue "yes."

Exercises

1. Find a firm that has exhibited smooth earnings growth for the past decade or so. How do you think this firm was able to have such smooth earnings? Find another firm that exhibited erratic earnings. Why do you think this firm was unable to show smooth earnings? Do some research and try to figure out what the repercussions have been to the latter firm for having erratic earnings.
2. When firms report their income to their shareholders, they want to show high income. When firms report their income to the IRS, they want to report low income. Find and describe three legal ways in which accountants are able to report different incomes to shareholders and to the IRS.
3. Periodically a firm might decide that its recent past financial statements did not accurately reflect its financial condition. When the firm provides a new revised financial statement, it is said to have restated. The number of earnings restatements has dramatically changed over the past decade. Do some research and try to figure out how and why the number has changed.
4. WorldCom disclosed that roughly $3.8 billion had been improperly booked as capital investments instead of operating expenses. Describe how this affected its financial statements, stock price, and credit rating.
5. Find a recent restatement announcement by a firm not discussed in this chapter. Describe the restatement and describe how it changes the firm's overall financial condition.
6. Do some research and try to identify some key differences between International Accounting Standards and U.S. GAAP.

Exercises for Non-U.S. Students

1. Do some research and describe the accounting principles in your country. How are they different from U.S. GAAP?

2. Describe some details of the external auditing system used in your country. Is there a designation similar to a CPA in your country? Does your country have similar problems with external auditing that the U.S. has? Whether you answer "yes" or "no" to this last question, describe and explain why.

3. To what extent are financial statements important in your country? Who uses financial statements the most? Investors? Lenders? Government?

4. To what extent does accounting manipulation occur in your country? Do you trust the accuracy of financial statements in your country? Elaborate on your answer.

5. How is accounting and auditing regulated in your country? Describe the regulatory body and its composition and describe its powers.

6. How would you improve the auditing environment in your country? Make sure you weigh the costs and benefits to your ideas. Also make sure you describe how your ideas are feasible.

Endnotes

1. There are limitations on how different public reporting and IRS reporting can be.

2. Susan Pulliam and Deborah Solomon, "How Three Unlikely Sleuths Exposed Fraud at WorldCom," *Wall Street Journal*, October 30, 2002, page 1.

3. Some of this discussion, along with some discussion in the section on managing earnings, comes from Steve Albrecht, James Stice, Earl Stice, and Monte Swain, *Accounting*, 9th edition, Thomson South-Western Publishing.

4. *www.gm.com/company/investor_ information/docs/fin_data/gm04ar/ content/financials/mar/mar_04.html*.

5. Jon Birger, "Glowing Numbers," *Money Magazine* (November 2000): 112–122.

6. Spencer Ante and David Henry, "Can IBM Keep Earnings Hot?" *Business Week* (April 15, 2002): 58–60.

7. Jesse Drucker and Henny Sender, 2002, "Sorry, Wrong Number: Strategy Behind Accounting Scheme," *Wall Street Journal*, June 27, page A9.

8. Paul Krugman, 2002, "Flavors of Fraud," *New York Times*, June 28, page A27, and "Everyone is Outraged," *New York Times*, July 2, page A21.

9. Reuters, "SEC Charges Ex-Rite Aid Execs with Fraud" (June 21, 2002): 11:05 a.m.

10. Rite Aid Corporation, Accounting and Auditing Enforcement Release No. 1579, *Securities and Exchange Commission*, June 21, 2002.

11. John Byrne, "Inside McKinsey," *Business Week* (July 8, 2002): 66–76.

12. William Symonds, "The Tax Games Tyco Played," *Business Week* (July 1, 2002): 40–41.

13. Christian Leuz, Dhananjay Nanda, and Peter Wysocki, "Investor Protection and Earnings Management: An International Comparison," *Journal of Financial Economics* 69, no. 3 (2003): 505–527.

4

THE BOARD
OF DIRECTORS

What are the responsibilities of a board of directors? In general, a board of directors is charged with the following five broad functions:

1. to hire, evaluate, and perhaps even fire top management, with the position of CEO being the most important to consider;
2. to vote on major operating proposals (e.g. large capital expenditures and acquisitions);
3. to vote on major financial decisions (e.g. issuance of stocks and bonds, dividend payments, and stock repurchases);
4. to offer expert advice to management; and
5. to make sure the firm's activities and financial condition are accurately reported to its shareholders.

In executing all of the above functions, directors are supposed to represent the interests of the shareholders. Therefore the board provides an important corporate governance function. Because the board is a part of the firm's organizational structure at the top of the corporate heirarchy it might be considered the firm's most important internal monitor.

While the board's role in the corporation seems to ensure that shareholder interests are being attended to, there are some potentially serious problems. Among the issues are a lack of board independence from the CEO, directors who do not have the time or expertise to fulfill their roles adequately, and members who do not have a vested interest in the firm. This chapter provides an overview of corporate boards and their role in corporate governance and it also highlights potential problems with many of today's boards.

OVERVIEW OF BOARDS

The Board's Legal Duties
No federal law explicitly dictates that public corporations must have a board of directors. Instead, corporations must follow the statute of the state in which they are incorporated. State laws vary from one state to the other but fortunately

every state requires that a corporation have a board of directors. The **Model Business Corporation Act** provides a guideline that states, "All corporate powers shall be exercised by or under authority of, and the business affairs of a corporation shall be managed under the direction of a board of directors." Further, all state laws abide by a concept known as the **business judgement rule**. Specifically, directors must act in good faith and with sincere belief that their actions are in the corporation's and shareholders' best interests. In order to abide by the spirit of this rule, directors have certain responsibilities, otherwise known as **duties**.

Because directors are supposed to represent shareholders' interests, directors have a **fiduciary duty** to conduct activities to enhance the firm's profitability and share value. Related to their fiduciary duty, directors also have a **duty of loyalty and fair dealing**, where they must put the interests of shareholders before their own *individual* interests. In addition, directors must also exercise a **duty of care** by doing what an ordinary prudent person would do under the same position and circumstances. Excercising this duty involves being informed and making rational decisions. Finally, the board of directors has a **duty of supervision**, in which they should establish rules of ethics and ensure disclosure. In this regard the board should hold regular meetings to review the firm's performance, operations, and management, and it must make sure that accurate financial reporting and objective auditing are taking place.

Board Committees

A great deal of important board work occurs at the subcommittee level and subsequently goes to the full board for approval. Some boards include an **executive committee**, a **finance committee**, a **community relations committee**, and a **corporate governance committee**, among others. The most common board subcommittees are the following:[1]

- audit committee
- compensation committee
- nomination committee

The audit committee is charged with finding an independent auditor for the firm's accounting statements and the committee must ensure that the auditor will do its job objectively. The compensation committee is responsible for setting and designing the executive compensation package. The nomination committee searches for and nominates candidates to run for impending vacancies among board seats in annual shareholder elections. A separate **stock options subcommittee** has gained popularity with boards in recent years, probably due to the controversy surrounding stock options.

Board Structure Regulations Imposed by Exchanges and the Sarbanes-Oxley Act

The stock exchanges New York Stock Exchange (NYSE) and NASDAQ—which as self-regulatory organizations (SROs) can impose their own set of regulations—require that their listed firms have an audit committee consisting primarily of independent directors. Since the scandals of 2001 and 2002, the exchanges have revised their regulations regarding the structure and function of a board of directors and the incentives provided to its members. Specifically, the NYSE mandates that companies have a majority of independent directors. A director is not independent if he (or immediate family) has worked for the company or its auditor within the past five years. Board members who are not also executives of the company must meet regularly without the presence of management.

The NYSE also requires specific functions of the board. For example, the nominating committee of the board must be composed entirely of independent directors and must perform certain duties. The same holds true of the compensation committee. Otherwise executives would have undue influence over their own compensation. The audit committee must also be independent; however, the members of this committee have an increased authority and responsibility to hire and fire the auditing firm. To handle this expanded responsibility, audit committee members must have the necessary experience and expertise in finance and accounting. To help maintain the independence of the audit committee, these board members may not receive compensation from the company, especially consulting fees, other than their regular director fees.

In the summer of 2002, the **Sarbanes-Oxley Act**, otherwise known as the **Public Company Accounting Reform and Investor Protection Act of 2002**, was passed. One section of the bill attempts to increase the monitoring ability and responsibilities of boards of directors and to improve their credibility. Specifically, the law makes the audit committee of the board of directors both more independent from management and more responsible for the hiring and oversight of auditing services and the accounting complaint process. More details of this Act are discussed in Chapter 10.

EXAMPLE 4.1

HISTORICAL PERSPECTIVE – IS A DIRECTOR SIMPLY A FIGURE-HEAD?

In 1934, William O. Douglas, a law professor who later served as an SEC chairman, and then as a U.S. Supreme Court justice for 36 years, claimed that directors do not direct. For the most part, his assertion has held true for some time. One director boasted in 1962, "If you have five directorships, it is total heaven, like having a permanent hot bath. No effort of any kind is called for. You go to a meeting once a month in a car supplied by the company, you look grave and sage, and on two occasions say, 'I agree.'"[2] For many years, a board of directors may have simply been something that corporations had for show rather than for a real purpose.

MORE ATTENTION ON DIRECTORS

Prior to the mid-1980s, the public paid little heed to directors and thought them merely ornamental features of corporations. However, the situation has changed. Increased pressure on the board of directors to provide better corporate governance possibly began as a response to the tidal wave of mergers and acquisitions (M&A) activity of the 1980s. A recession and the collapse of the junk bond market resulted in a temporary M&A decline during the late 1980s, but M&A activity was strong again in the 1990s. In fact, since the mid-1990s, M&A activity has taken off in the U.S. Some of the largest mergers ever have taken place in the last 10 years.

Why would an increase in M&A activity lead to more board scrutiny? When one firm acquires another, it usually has to pay significantly more than the going market price. This situation is advantageous for the target firm's shareholders but not for the acquiring firm's shareholders. The boards of both firms must approve the acquisition before it goes to a shareholder vote. For the acquirer, the shareholders may not wish to pay too much for a target, or may not wish to acquire the target at all. For the target firm, the shareholders may want to make sure that firm is acquired for a nice price, or perhaps not acquired at all. Consequently, the shareholders of both the potential acquirers and targets keep a close eye on their respective boards during a prospective takeover.

Boards of directors also received more scrutiny from shareholders because of two rules adopted by the SEC in 1992. First, the SEC required additional disclosure from corporations with regard to executive compensation, including the reporting of granted stock option values. When the values of these compensation contracts were disclosed, shareholders learned that CEOs were receiving millions of dollars per year in salary, bonuses, and stock options. In many cases, lavish compensation was granted, even if the firm was not doing that well or was unprofitable. As such, shareholders began pressuring directors to make sure that the executives deserved what they were earning. The SEC also made it easier for shareholders to communicate with one another. Large institutional investors such as the pension funds California Public Employees' Retirement System (CalPERS) and Teachers Insurance and Annuity Association—College Retirement Equities Fund (TIAA-CREF) took advantage of this rule. As a result, they were able to create stronger shareholder coalitions that in turn made it easier to put pressure on boards to challenge management. Institutional shareholder activism will be discussed in a later chapter.

The increased takeover market and the new regulatory environment for shareholder communication caused shareholders and the general public to put more pressure on directors to do their jobs. However, because these changes occurred or took shape only recently, the avid attention being paid to boards is a recent phenomenon. For example, *Business Week* only started rating corporate boards in 1996.

EXAMPLE 4.2

WHO ARE DIRECTORS?

Standard & Poor's 500 firms have about 11 directors each. How are these 5,500 or so board seats filled? The people nominated by the firm's management or board's nominating committee often become directors. University deans or presidents and politicians are viewed as respectable figureheads but most directors are executives of other firms. For example, Korn/Ferry states that a person would have to possess 10 to 20 years of experience in a business leadership role, be a current COO or CFO of a large company, or be one of the top 15 executives at a very large corporation, to be considered a viable candidate for director. Sometimes a large individual shareholder submits a proposal to obtain a board seat. If the person is well-known or wealthy enough to launch an expensive campaign, he might gather enough votes to be elected.

According to the 2004 Korn/Ferry study, 95 percent of Fortune 1000 firms have a retired executive serving as a director, 82 percent have an executive from another firm, 58 percent have an academic, and 58 percent have a former government official. With regard to gender and race representation, board diversity seems to be improving. Eighty-two percent of boards have a woman as a director and 76 percent have a member of an ethnic minority, with African Americans sitting on 47 percent of our nation's boards. These are large increases from 1995, when 69 percent of the boards had a woman and 47 percent had an ethnic minory, with 34 percent being African American.

EXAMPLE 4.3

IS BEING A DIRECTOR WORTH IT?

During the past 15 years or so, shareholders have become increasingly more demanding of directors and, as a result, directors have been working longer hours, taking more stock ownership in the firm to ensure a vested interest, challenging the CEO more often, and taking their duties more seriously. These demands are starting to take their toll on directors.

According to recruiters Christian & Timbers, 60 percent of nominated directors are turning down appointments. Nonetheless, with director compensation averaging more than $56,000 per year—along with perks, travel, stocks, and stock options—all for working about 150 hours and attending eight meetings a year, directorship is lucrative.[3]

WHAT IS A "GOOD" BOARD?

Of course, boards that have members who have relevant experience and expertise are likely to be good boards. A board of a manufacturing firm probably should include someone who has worked in the same or similar industry for many years and has achieved some success in it. A board that consists of members that have different backgrounds may also be a good board. For example, the same manufacturing firm could benefit from someone who has marketing experience and from someone who has accounting experience. Each firm may need to decide for themselves what kind of background, experience, and expertise would serve the board and the firm optimally. But let us assume that all public firms have experienced and successful experts serving on their boards, currently a reasonable assumption. After all, if one looks at any board of a random large firm in the U.S. (and probably in any country), one will often find that the board consists of recognizable and successful business leaders and experts. If all boards consist of proven business leaders and business experts, then what might make one board better than another? We discussed earlier that there is increasing emphasis on having independent boards. In addition, perhaps small boards are better than large boards. We discuss each in turn next.

Independent Boards

There is a general consensus that when a board has a higher fraction of non-insiders (otherwise known as outside or independent directors), then it is presumed to be more effective at monitoring management. The logic is pretty straight-forward. For example, one of the board's primary responsibilities is to evaluate, compensate, and possibly fire the CEO. What if the board consists of the following people: the firm's CFO, a friend of the CEO, a relative of the CEO, and a business collaborator of the CEO? This board is probably less likely to fire the CEO for poor performance. For this reason shareholders and regulators generally believe that outside directors are more objective at evaluating management. Research from academia confirms this intuition. When firms do poorly, the firms with a higher fraction of independent board members are more likely to fire the CEO.[4]

However, in today's business world, is it possible to find people who are entirely and unambiguously independent of the firm's management? For example, it may be unlikely to expect that two industry experts do not know one another personally. Also the definition of an independent versus inside director is not a black or white issue. A board member could be a cousin of the CEO or former employee of the CEO from another firm. These types of directors might be considered independent by the firm's management, but are they really? Because all directors may simply be a different shade of gray with regard to their independence stature, it makes it difficult for academic researchers to identify a relation between board independence and board effectiveness. This also makes it difficult for regulators to impose board independence regulations, as what is deemed independent is ambiguous.

Small Boards

A board with fewer members might be a better board. This view might be counter-intuitive to some but not to others (think about how the American colloquialisms "more the merrier" and "too many cooks spoil the broth" both convey a supposed truism and yet represent opposite thinking). However, there is some research that has shown that smaller boards are more effective at enhancing a firm's value than larger boards.[5] The logic for why this might be deals with the free-rider problem. For a board with few directors, each board member may feel inclined to exert more effort than they would have otherwise, as they each realize that there are only a few others monitoring the firm. With larger boards, each member may simply assume that the many other members are monitoring. Further, with larger boards, it may be more difficult to reach consensus and thus to get anything meaningful done. Therefore, smaller boards may be more dynamic and more active.

Board Structure in the U.S. and Around the World

Figure 4.1 shows the average number of independent (outside) and inside directors for U.S. companies grouped by firm size and various industries.[6] While there appears to be some variation in the average board size, all industries show a large portion of independent directors. The average board size for all U.S. companies is 10, with 8 being independent.

Figure 4.2 shows the size and composition of boards in six countries as reported in the 2004 Korn/Ferry Annual Board of Directors Survey. Australia, France, and the U.K. have a majority of independent directors, while Germany

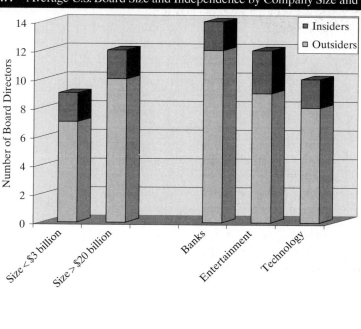

FIGURE 4.1   Average U.S. Board Size and Independence by Company Size and Industry

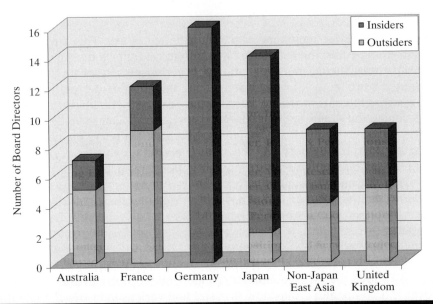

FIGURE 4.2   Average Board Size and Independence, 2004

and East Asia companies have a majority of insider directors. German boards have all insider directors. Boards in Australia, Non-Japan East Asia,[7] and the U.K. have smaller boards (nine members or less) on average. Obviously, not all countries share the U.S.'s emphasis on independent directors. In addition, companies in different countries also seem to have differing views on board size.

Good for the Goose, Good for the Gander?

If independent boards are objective and if small boards are more active, then it would be tempting to conclude that all firms should have independent and small boards. What is good for one firm must be good for all firms. However, this may not be the case. Recall that we mentioned earlier that firms might have to decide what experience and expertise is optimal for their firm. This may hold true for board independence and board size. For example, a young growth-oriented firm may actually need more insiders, not outside-independent directors. If a firm's primary product is unique, then the firm's own employees might be the best people to serve on the board. Larger and more diversified firms may need more directors, not fewer directors, given the scale and diversified scope of its operations. From Figures 4.1 and 4.2, it even appears that some countries are inclined toward having more inside directors, and more directors overall, than other countries. Maybe for those countries, their board structures are best suited for their particular operating or legal environment.

Without specific regulations pertaining to board composition and size, each firm would be able to decide on its own what is the best board. However, who should make this decision? The firm's manager? He may be in the best position to pick a good board but his self-interests may get in the way. The firm's outside shareholders? Though they have the legal power to vote on board members, they may not have the power to appoint directors if they are unable to form a majority consensus. Also, while outsiders are more likely to be objective in appointing directors, they may be less qualified. Of course, there could be stricter regulations pertaining to board composition and size but this would take away some of the firm's flexibility to form boards best suited for them.

Can Good Boards Lead to Better Firm Performance?

While independent boards and small boards might be better at monitoring the firm and the firm's managers, it is not clear that there is a positive correlation between board quality and firm performance. When one firm out-performs another, how can we tell if the board had anything to do with the performance difference? In professional sports, it is often difficult to single out who is to blame when a team does not have a winning season. Is it the players, the coaches, the executives, or the owners? While good boards may be good at fixing serious problems (in other words, they may be effectively reactive), they may not be good at creating value (in other words, they may not be effectively proactive).

Academic research echoes these dual sentiments. Most scholars agree that independent boards are more likely than inside directors to fire a CEO after a serious firm performance decline. However, academic researchers are almost equally divided on whether or not board quality and firm performance are positively related.

What might matter, when it comes to board compositions, is identifying which specific board committees are best served by independent directors and which may not be. For example, committees that determine CEO compensation and are responsible for the firm's audit may best be served by outsiders, but committees that make firm financing and long-term investment decisions may be served best by insiders.[8] Note from our previous discussion pertaining to recently adopted board structure regulations that regulators seem to agree with this viewpoint also.

POTENTIAL PROBLEMS WITH TODAY'S BOARDS

As already mentioned, one of the main functions of the board is to evaluate top management, especially the CEO. However, for many firms, the board's chairman is also the firm's CEO. Among the 30 firms that are included in the Dow Jones Industrial Average, which consists of the U.S.'s major corporations, only 10 firms have a separate CEO and board chair. For the Fortune-listed firms, only 10 percent have a non-executive chairman. Therefore the same person who manages the firm also runs the board meetings and its agenda and is consequently the one who controls the information given to the board. This being the case, is the board capable of seriously evaluating or challenging the CEO? We mentioned that it can happen but often only as a result of significant shareholder pressure.

Even if the CEO is not the board chair, he is not necessarily under a more careful watch. While most boards have more outsiders than insiders, we mentioned before that many of these so-called outside board members might have some sort of business or personal tie to the CEO.

The boards of firms that have been reeling from scandal (e.g. Tyco, Global Crossings, and Adelphia) were filled with former or current executives. Further, one of Tyco's outside directors was paid $10 million for helping to arrange the acquisition of CIT Group. Former Adelphia CEO John Rigas, along with his three sons, held four out of the nine board seats. Can this quartet be expected to be objective monitors?

Another problem with some boards is that directors do not have a significant vested interest in the firm. For example, most of Disney's outside directors own little or no stock. In 1997, *Business Week* reported that the Occidental Petroleum board had approved a $95 million payout to its CEO but two of its board members, George O. Nolley and Aziz D. Syriani, only owned 2,280 and 1,450 shares of the firm's stocks, respectively, despite the fact that they had sat on the board for

EXAMPLE 4.4

DISNEY'S BOARD DURING THE 1990S

The Walt Disney Company CEO is Michael Eisner. As such he is supposed to be monitored by Disney's board of directors. However, Disney's board has been criticized by *Business Week* as one of the worst in corporate America and it has consisted of numerous current Disney managers, such as the chief corporate officer (CCO) and heads of various Disney operations. Disney claims, however, that 13 of the 16 board members are independent directors. These "outsiders" include Reveta Bowers, headmaster of the school that Eisner's children attended; George Mitchell, a paid consultant to Disney and an attorney whose law firm represents Disney; Stanley Gold, president of Shamrock Holdings, which manages investments for the Disney family;

Leo O'Donovan, president of Georgetown University, which one of the Eisner children attended and which received donations from Eisner; Irwin Russell, Eisner's personal attorney; and Robert Stern, architect for several Disney projects.

Will Disney's board challenge Eisner? Not only do some of these directors work for Eisner but there are obviously others who also benefit from not angering him. In other words, this board has too many insiders and those with business or other vested interests with the CEO. A lucrative contract penned for Eisner netted him more than $700 million in the last years of the 1990s. Disney's market value fell to less than half of what it was during the run-up of the 1990s.

14 years.[9] The article also reported that Advanced Micro Devices director Charles M. Blalack and Microsoft director Richard Hackborn owned no shares of their firm. Can these board members empathize with their shareholders? Probably not.

However, the situation has been changing. For example, some firms, such as Ashland Inc., are setting stock ownership targets for their directors. To Eisner's credit, he has asked his directors to own more stock. For GE, the outside directors are clearly aligned with shareholders, as they owned (at the beginning of the year 2000), an average of $6.6 million of GE stock each.[10] According to the 2004 Korn/Ferry study, 65 percent of the directors were required to own some of the board's company stock.

Are directors capable of providing the time and expertise required to fully understand the major operating and financial decisions of the firm? Some directors, especially those who are potentially good in that role, may be overextended. For example, many directors serve on multiple boards. According to a 1997 *Business Week* article, several people held directorships in 10 or more firms.[11] Coca-Cola has 5 directors (out of 13) who serve on at least 5 boards. In addition, most directors also have their own highly demanding full-time jobs. Often they are company executives themselves.

In addition, some directors simply do not have the expertise to be a board member. This means that independence, in and of itself, is not a sufficient quality for being an effective director. Some boards want to have a few figureheads, such as a celebrity (O.J. Simpson was once on the audit committee of Infinity Broadcasting) or a former army general but other candidates probably could offer more help to the firm.

Finally, as mentioned before, some boards are simply too large, which makes it more unlikely that all directors will be actively involved and more difficult to accomplish needed work. Disney's board has 16 members and Enron's had 15. Is this too large and is this part of the problem? Some academic researchers believe so. As mentioned before, according to some studies, firms with fewer directors have higher market values, indicating their effectiveness.

In summary, many potential problems plague boards today. Many directors might not be truly independent, they might be too busy, and they might not have the expertise to carry out their obligations. These problems might explain why some corporate scandals occur.

INTERNATIONAL PERSPECTIVE – BOARDS IN WESTERN EUROPE

Two-Tier Boards

Some European countries have firms with a two-tier board structure. For example, German firms have a management board that essentially runs the business and a supervisory board that appoints and supervises the management board. The supervisory board also controls the firm's compliance with the law and

EXAMPLE 4.5

IS ENRON'S BOARD PARTIALLY TO BLAME?

Enron's board, which consisted of 15 members, epitomized the notion of one that is "captive" to the firm's CEO. Board member John Wakeham was a British Conservative Party politician who had approved the building of an Enron power plant in Britain in 1990. Four years later Wakeham was on the Enron board. Director Herbert Winokur is chairman and CEO of Capricorn Holdings. He also sat on the board of National Tank Company, which sold equipment and services to Enron divisions for millions of dollars. Directors Charles LeMaistre and John Mendelsohn were former president and president, respectively, of the M. D. Anderson Cancer Center, which received more than $500 million from Enron and its chairman, Ken Lay, during a five-year period. Director Wendy Gramm, a former chairwoman of the Commodity Futures Trading Commission, backed several policies that benefited Enron and other energy trading companies before she joined the Enron board. Her husband, Senator Phil Gramm, is a major recipient of Enron campaign donations. Board member Robert Belfer is founder and former chairman and CEO of Belco Oil and Gas Corporation. Belco and Enron had numerous financial arrangements. Director Charles Walker is a tax lobbyist. Firms partly owned by Walker were paid more than $70,000 by Enron for consulting services. In addition, Enron also made donations to a nonprofit corporation chaired by Walker. A Senate report argues that the board failed in their fiduciary duties to represent shareholders and that the Enron failure was partly due to the lack of the board's independence.

In 1999, auditors had already told Enron board members that the company was using accounting practices that "push[ed] limits" and were "at the edge" of what was acceptable. One director, Robert Jaedicke, had been an accounting professor at Stanford University. Also the board knowingly allowed Enron to move more than half of its assets off the balance sheet. Governance experts used by the Senate investigation stated that this activity was unheard of but only one Enron board member expressed any concern when it was occurring. The board even waived a code of conduct stipulation for CFO Andrew Fastow, allowing him to create private offshore partnerships that would conduct business with Enron. Under the Enron code of conduct, no employee is allowed to obtain financial gain from an entity that does business with Enron. Under Fastow's watch, these entities profited at Enron's expense but the board idly sat by despite Fastow's obvious conflict of interest.

The Senate report concludes that the board missed a dozen red flags that should have warned them about possible shenanigans at the firm. For example, directors were told that in a six-month period, Fastow's partnerships had generated $2 billion in funds for Enron. While Enron's board apparently was not involved in the fraud, they should have put a stop to it.[12] After all, they were being paid more than $350,000 a year in salary, stocks, and stock options by Enron to be its directors. In the Senate report's conclusion, they state, "much that was wrong with Enron was known to the Board . . . By failing to provide sufficient oversight and restraint to stop management excess, the Enron Board contributed to the company's collapse and bears a share of the responsibility for it."[13]

A class-action lawsuit was filed by Enron's shareholders and in January 7, 2005, Enron directors agreed to pay $168 million as part of Enron's overall settlement with its shareholders. $13 million comes directly from the directors' pockets. Shareholders claimed that Enron directors sold shares after false financial statements were filed. Enron directors claimed no wrong-doing. Only a few days earlier, WorldCom announced that its directors agreed to a $54 million settlement with its shareholders, with directors being personally responsbile for $18 million of it. Traditionally, some have viewed the *business judgement rule* as being too lenient toward directors. That is, it is easy for directors to claim that they are doing the best that they can. Today, however, directors may be facing higher standards.

articles of the corporation and its business strategies. A person cannot belong to both boards. The Netherlands also has a two-tier board structure. Interestingly, in France, a firm can choose between having a one-tier or two-tier board structure but most choose the one-tier board. However, it could be argued that these two-tiered boards are similar to what the U.S. and the U.K. would deem as their top management and the board.

Board Regulations on Independence

As mentioned earlier, one of the primary issues pertaining to board quality and efficacy is board independence. Among Western European countries, the U.K. is probably most similar to the U.S. in its emphasis on independent directors. The U.K.'s *Combined Code on Corporate Governance*, released in July 2003, states that "Except for smaller companies, at least half the board, excluding the chairman, should comprise non-executive directors determined by the board to be independent." Before the passage of the Combined Code, the Cadbury Committee issued a *Code of Best Practice* recommending that each firm should have at least three independent directors. While it is too early to assess the 2003 Combined Code, there is some solid evidence that the Cadbury Committee's Code has been successful.[14]

However, the governance codes for the rest of the European countries do not explicitly require a specific number or fraction of independent directors. Instead they make "recommendations" or "suggestions" pertaining to independent directors. For example, the 1998 Cardon Report, commissioned by the Brussels Stock Exchange suggests that "The number of independent directors should be sufficient for their views to carry significant weight in the board's decisions." In the most recent version of Belgium's *Corporate Governance Act*, it states, "the composition of the board should be determined on the basis of the necessary diversity and complementarily." For France, the Viénot report of July 1999 recommends that at least a third of the directors be independent. Later, an October 2003 report, released by the French Association of Private Enterprise, "suggests" that for widely-held firms, at least half of its directors be independent. Italy's *Corporate Governance Code* of 2002 states that "an adequate number of non-executive directors shall be independent." Spain's *Aldama Report* of 2003 suggests "a very significant number of independent directors, considering the company's ownership structure and the capital represented on the Board."

Clearly, the wide attention on director independence is a recent phenomenon. Further, the recommendations pertaining to director independence with regard to their number and/or fraction seem vague and do not seem to be explicit regulations. Is it enough to merely advocate board independence or do there have to be explicit regulations and backing? For example, the Cadbury Report makes explicit recommendations but they are not explicit regulations, but because the London Stock Exchange specifically asks listing firms whether or not they are compliant with the Cadbury recommendations, these recommendations seem to have "teeth" and have been found to be successful in improving governance for U.K. firms.[15]

EXAMPLE 4.6

WESTERN EUROPEAN COUNTRIES THAT SEEM TO PLACE SOME SIGNIFICANT EMPHASIS ON BOARD INDEPENDENCE

Belgium	Denmark	France
Germany	Greece	Ireland
Italy	Netherlands	Portugal
Spain	United Kingdom	

(Note: exclusion from this list does not mean that the excluded country does not emphasize board independence):

Summary

A firm's board of directors plays an important role in reducing problems inherent in the separation of ownership and control. Indeed, the board is responsible for hiring, evaluating, and sometimes firing the firm's executives. In addition, the board oversees the firm's auditors and makes major strategic decisions for the firm. They are to conduct these activities in the best interests of the shareholders.

Shareholders and regulators have only recently started paying attention to the activities of boards of directors. There are many potential problems with the organization of many corporate boards. For example, it seems that many directors lack the independence, the vested interest, the time, and sometimes the expertise to carry out their fiduciary obligations to shareholders. Enron's board is a telling example. However, the recent attention directed to boards has caused some changes to occur (especially regulatory changes) but it is too early to tell if these changes are taking hold.

WEB Info about Boards of Directors

Korn/Ferry International
www.kornferry.com

The Corporate Library
www.thecorporatelibrary.com

European Corporate Governance Institute
www.ecgi.de

International Corporate Governance Network
www.icgn.org

Review Questions

1. What regulations govern the functions and structure of boards of directors? What is legally required of directors? What are the primary roles of boards and board sub-committees?
2. How did the increased merger activity in the 1980s increase the attention given to corporate boards?
3. Broadly speaking, what defines a good board? Do all firms benefit from this broad definition of a good board?
4. What is the relationship between board quality and firm monitoring, and between board quality and firm performance?
5. What are the main problems in modern boards? How might they be changed to fix those problems?
6. How are corporate boards of directors in Western Europe different from the U.S.?

Discussion Questions

1. How would you evaluate whether or not a board is doing a good job on a day-to-day basis? Also, how would you apply the *business judgement rule* standard on directors?
2. If you were the largest outside shareholder of General Motors, who would you want on your board and why? If you are the largest outside shareholder of a firm that operates an

internet search engine that just recently went public, who would you want on your board and why?

3. Should there be regulations pertaining to board composition and structure? If you think so, then what kind of regulations?

4. As a potential investor of a stock, do you think it would be worthwhile to examine the firm's board before purchasing its stock? What would you look for?

Exercises

1. In the state you are in right now, find and describe the state laws pertaining to corporate boards.
2. Examine the 30 firms in the Dow Jones Industrial Average. Which firms have the same person holding the CEO and board chairman titles? Are certain types of firms more likely to have a CEO/Chairman?
3. Pick a company and identify all the board directors, their affiliation, and their compensation from the directorship. Much of this information can be obtained from proxy statements the firm files with the SEC.

4. Find three recent cases where the CEO of a firm was fired. What happened?
5. In the summer of 2002, WorldCom declared bankruptcy. It was the largest bankruptcy in history. A class-action lawsuit was filed by sharehodlers and subsequently settled. Investigate what happened to WorldCom and how its board of directors was complicit in WorldCom's problems.
6. In 2005, Walt Disney shareholders lost their long-running lawsuit against their board's hiring, firing, and compensating of Michael Ovitz, former President of Walt Disney. Describe the surrounding details and circumstances.

Exercises for Non-U.S. Students

1. Try to identify the board members of a public firm from your native country. In what way is the board composition and structure similar to and/or different from a comparable U.S. firm? Why do you think these similarities and/or differences exist?

2. What are the regulations pertaining to boards, if any, in your native country? Why do these regulations exist (or not exist)? In your opinion, do you think these regulations (or lack of regulations) are appropriate for your country?

Endnotes

1. 31st Annual Board of Directors Study, Korn/Ferry International, (Los Angeles, CA, 2004).
2. Katrina Brooker, "Trouble in the Boardroom," *Fortune* (May 13, 2002): 113–116.
3. These statistics are based on averages reported in the 31st Annual Board of Directors Study, Korn/Ferry International, 2004.

4. Jerold B. Warner, Ross L. Watts, and Karen H. Wruck, "Stock Prices and Top Management Changes," *Journal of Financial Economics* 20 (1989): 461–492; Michael S. Weisback, "Outside Directors and CEO Turnover," *Journal of Financial Economics* 20 (1988): 431–460; Kenneth A. Borokhovich, Robert Parrino, and Teresa Trapani, "Outside

Directors and CEO Selection," *Journal of Financial and Quantitative Analysis* 31, no. 3 (1996): 337–355; Kathleen A. Farrell and David A. Whidbee, "The Consequences of Forced CEO Succession for Outside Directors," *The Journal of Business* 73, no. 4, (2000): 597–627.

5. Jeff Huther, "An Empirical Test of the Effect of Board Size on Firm Efficiency," *Economics Letters* 54, no. 3, (1996): 259–264; David Yermack, "Higher Market Valuation of Companies with a Small Board of Directors", *Journal of Financial Economics* 40, no. 2 (1996): 185–211.

6. Data is from the 31st Annual Board of Directors Study, Korn/Ferry International, (Los Angeles, CA, 2004).

7. Non-Japan East Asia firms are China (including Hong Kong), Malaysia, Singapore, and Thailand.

8. April Klein, "Firm Performance and Board Committee Structure," *Journal of Law and Economics* 41 (April 1998): 275–303.

9. "Directors in the Hot Seat," *Business Week* (December 8, 1997): 100–104.

10. "The Best and Worst Corporate Boards," *Business Week* (January 24, 2000) from *www.businessweek.com*.

11. John A. Byrne, Leslie Brown, and Joyce Barnathan, "Directors in the Hot Seat," *Business Week* (December 8, 1997): 100–104.

12. John Byrne, "Commentary: No Excuses for Enron's Board," *Business Week* (July 29, 2002) from *www.businessweek.com*.

13. Source: "The Role of the Board of Directors in Enron's Collapse," U.S. Senate Report 107–170, July 8, 2002.

14. Jay Dahya, John J. McConnell, and Nickolaos G. Travlos, "The Cadbury Committee, Corporate Performance, and Top Management Turnover," *Journal of Finance* 57, no. 1 (2002): 461–483.

15. Jay Dahya, John J. McConnell, and Nickolaos G. Travlos, "The Cadbury Committee, Corporate Performance, and Top Management Turnover," *Journal of Finance* 57, no. 1 (2002): 461–483.

5

INVESTMENT BANKS AND SECURITIES ANALYSTS

This chapter deals with investment banks and securities analysts. Investment banks offer a variety of services but their most notable business is selling newly-created securities. When a private firm wants to become a public firm, it will obtain the services of an investment bank to design and to sell the new stocks for the investing public to purchase. When an already public firm wants to raise additional capital to finance its on-going activities or future growth, it will also obtain the services of an investment bank to sell its newly-created securities to the public. One can think of investment banks as intermediaries who sell new securities on behalf of firms.

The primary job of analysts is to evaluate securities and then to make buy and/or sell recommendations to their clients based on their evaluations. Analysts are also expected to make earnings forecasts for the firms that they follow in order to help investors make their own buy and/or sell decisions.

Most corporate governance texts might not consider investment banks and securities analysts as part of the corporate governance system. However, because investment banks evaluate their client firms' needs and bring investment opportunities to the market and because analysts frequently possess better information than most investors about a company, both investment banks and analysts are in a good position to monitor the firm and to identify problems for shareholders. We would expect investment bankers to sell "good" securities (i.e. they should not be selling securities of a poorly run firm) and for analysts to recommend "good" securities (i.e. they should not be recommending stocks that they think will go down in value). Therefore, they both do represent an important and integral part of the corporate governance system. This chapter first discusses investment banks and then it discusses analysts.

INVESTMENT BANKING ACTIVITIES

The basic investment banking service is to help companies issue new debt and equity securities. A firm can issue several different kinds of securities. The bank advises the company on the optimal security (stocks, bonds, etc.) for the amount of capital being raised, while taking into account the company's situation. The investment banks charge the company a fee for this service. The size of the fee depends on how much risk the investment bank takes to issue the securities. There are two methods that banks can use to issue stock and bonds: underwriting and best efforts.

Think about the case of issuing stock. When **underwriting** an issue, the bank will guarantee that the company will receive a specific amount of capital. That is, the banker assures the company that a certain number of shares will sell at a target price. If too few shares sell at that price, the investment bank must buy those shares. For example, if a bank guarantees that it will be able to raise $100 million in capital for the issuing firm but is only able to sell $70 million worth of stock, then the bank would have to buy $30 million worth of stock. The fee for underwriting a $100 million issue is typically about $7 million for a new issue (i.e. for an initial public offering or IPO) and $5 million for issues raised by already existing public companies (i.e. for a seasoned equity offering or SEO).

If the investment bank did not want to assume the risk on a security issue, it could use the **best-efforts** method. Here the bank does not guarantee that the firm will get its desired amount of capital. The bank does its best to sell as much of the new security as possible for the company. In this case the company takes the risk of not receiving enough capital. Because the risk is low for the investment bank, the fee charged is much lower for the best-efforts method than for underwriting.

The process of selling securities to public investors first involves registering securities with the SEC (more about this in the SEC chapter). The document submitted to the SEC includes a preliminary prospectus containing information about the security issue and the company. For example, the prospectus details the company's financial condition, business activities, management experience, and how the funds raised will be used. The bank distributes the final prospectus to investors interested in the securities issue. Note that this information helps investors make decisions about the condition of the company and about buying the issue. In other words, investment bankers are an important source of information and monitoring of a public company.

The prospectus and the banker's "road show" relay information about the company to investors. The road show is the marketing campaign done by bankers to generate interest and to market the issue. They travel the country visiting large institutional investors such as public pension funds and mutual funds. To sell to individual investors, investment banks use their brokerage operations. For a "hot" issue, investors call the brokers to order shares. In a less popular issue, the brokers call investors.

Information about the issuing company is especially important to investors when the firm is new. When a firm offers stock to the public for the first time in an IPO, the company is typically young, small, and mostly unknown to investors. The information gathered by the investment bank and presented to the SEC may be the only independent data available on the firm. Therefore investors expect the bank to disclose all relevant information in order to make good investment decisions.

Investment banks experience greater risk when underwriting an IPO, as opposed to underwriting an SEO, because of the uncertainty involved with new firms. To mitigate some of the risk, banks tend to underprice IPO offerings. That is, banks offer the new shares of stock at a lower price than the demand for the stock would suggest. For example, on July 25, 2002, the newly public firm LeapFrog Enterprises conducted an IPO to raise $130 million. The company produces technology-enhanced toys and is considered a business of Michael Milken, the junk bond king of the 1980s. A syndicate of banks conducted the underwriting services for this deal and those investors who purchased the stock from these investment banks bought it at $13 per share. However, there were not enough shares for all the investors who wanted them and the investors who were left out of the deal had to buy shares on the New York Stock Exchange (NYSE) later that day. On the first day that LeapFrog's stock traded on the NYSE, the stock price opened at $15.50 per share and closed the day at $15.85. The first-day return for the stock was 22 percent. The investment banks were probably well aware that the first-day trading price would be greater than $13 per share but they underpriced the stock offer anyway to ensure that they would sell all of the stock and reduce their liability to LeapFrog.

Underpricing IPOs lowers the risk to the underwriters and makes the new issues highly desirable to investors. After all, who would not want a 22 percent return in one day? Figure 5.1 shows the number of IPOs offered in each year

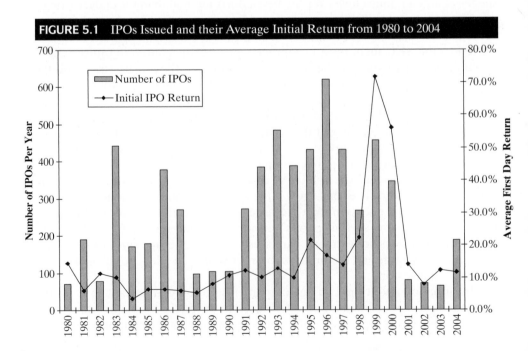

FIGURE 5.1 IPOs Issued and their Average Initial Return from 1980 to 2004

from 1980 to 2004.[1] The line represents the average first-day return for the offerings each year. Note that the average first-day return is positive in every year but that does not mean that every IPO experiences a price increase on the first day. Some IPOs are in high demand and earn a positive return—others are in low demand and decline in price the first day. The average initial return for IPOs in the late 1990s and 2000 was extraordinarily high. The average in 1999 was more than 70 percent! During the 1990s, the average underpricing in the U.S. was just over 20 percent. This compares to 16.5 percent in France, 40.2 percent in Germany, and 39.6 percent in the U.K.[2]

CRITICISMS OF INVESTMENT BANKS

IPO Problems

Investment banks take small private firms public in IPOs. These small firms want to expand using the capital that the stock issue provides. Every small business owner would like to gain tens or hundreds of millions of dollars to spend, but few small businesses would make good public companies. That is, the business model of many small firms would not work effectively as large, national firms. In addition, small business owners may not be capable of running a large business.

Typically, only a small fraction (less than 1 percent) of firms that want to conduct an IPO actually do. Who decides which firms go public? Investment banks make this decision. After all, they take the risk as the underwriters. The banks thoroughly examine potential IPO firms. Traditionally, the policy of many banks has been to bring a firm public only if it has put together a good management team, developed a quality business plan, and perfected its business model enough so that it has earned profits in the past three quarters. The companies brought public from 1986 to 1995 experienced only a 1 percent failure rate.[3] This rate is defined as the firm's stock price falling to less than $1 (or delisted from the exchanges) within the first three years after the IPO. Investment banks did a good job of offering quality companies to investors during the late 1980s to the mid-1990s. As such they provided an important monitoring service to the investment community.

The situation began to change in the mid- to late-1990s. The stock prices of technology firms dramatically increased and were enormously popular with investors. The demand from investors for more technology stocks seemed insatiable. Hundreds of millions of dollars were to be made by taking tech firms public. The investment banking industry raked in more than $2 billion in banking fees. There were not enough new firms that met the traditionally high quality standards of the banks but investors did not seem to care. They seemed to want any new tech stock at any price. Notice how high the average first day returns of IPOs were in 1999 and 2000. The risk of underwriting these firms did not seem very high with such strong demand. To meet the high demand, banks began to bring inferior companies to the market.

EXAMPLE 5.1

PETS.COM INITIAL PUBLIC OFFERING

Consider the IPO of Pets.com. In 1999, the firm had only $5.8 million in revenue and reported an operating loss of $61.8 million. Yet Merrill Lynch launched the Pets.com IPO in February 2000. The firm raised $66 million in capital and Merrill received more than $4 million in fees.[4] Ten months later, Pets.com filed for bankruptcy and folded.

The firms that offered IPOs in the period 1998 to 2000 experienced a 12 percent failure rate, which is much higher than the historic 1 percent rate. Investment banks apparently lost their desire to be gatekeepers of quality firms and monitors for investors. Investors probably measure success differently; they measure it by their investment return. Of the 367 Internet firms that have gone public since 1997, only 15 percent have made money compared to their offer prices. More than 200 firms have lost more than 75 percent of their value. What made this even worse for individual investors is that the average investor rarely can access good IPOs at the offer price. Instead such investors usually cannot buy the stock until it starts trading on the stock exchange. By then the stock has typically already increased in price. Consequently, poor returns are even worse for the average individual investor.

Structured Deals

When companies need more capital, they turn to investment banks. Raising capital can be difficult. As an extreme example, consider a firm facing bankruptcy. In bankruptcy, the equity of the firm is taken from the stockholders, who gain nothing, and given to some of the creditors. Therefore investors are not likely to buy additional shares of a financially troubled firm. The firm would also have trouble borrowing money from banks or from bond investors because these creditors typically do not recoup all their money in the bankrutpcy court.

Often a firm has trouble raising capital, even if it is not on the brink of bankruptcy. For example, the current creditors of the firm may have stipulated in their loans that the firm cannot borrow more money unless they are repaid first. Also few firms can successfully issue additional stock when investor confidence is low, as it has been since the early 2000s.

One criticism of investment banks is that they sometimes have been active participants in helping companies raise capital outside traditional avenues, thus manipulating earnings. Enron's strategy was to launch structured deals using special purpose entities (SPEs) created in tax havens such as the Cayman Islands. The SPEs were formed as partnerships that created the appearance of third-party companies doing business with Enron. The "business" actually turned out to be loans that were not recorded as debt but instead, recorded as revenue. For the structured deals to work, Enron needed complicated structures to fool auditors and regulators. To help create and fund the deals, Enron turned to investment banks. Large institutional investors frequently funded these partnerships.

EXAMPLE 5.2

ENRON'S PARTNERSHIPS

Enron invested heavily in an internet start-up called Rhythms NetConnections. Rhythms stock had jumped and the investment of $10 million grew to $300 million, a $290 million profit! Due to restrictions on selling ownership in the recent IPO, Enron could not sell this stock right away. Because of its mark-to-market method of accounting, Enron could book the gain. However, Enron worried that a big decline in price later would require booking a large loss.[5] Enron could not persuade investment banks to hedge the price risk because of Enron's huge position in the high-risk start-up Rhythms. Consequently, Enron created a partnership called LJM in the Cayman Islands that would guarantee the profit.[6] Enron CFO Andrew Fastow would run the partnership. The new partnership was funded by Enron stock. Therefore Enron was really insuring itself. The Rhythms profit would represent 30 percent of Enron's total profit for the year. The danger was that if both Rhythms stock and the Enron stock price fell, LJM would not have enough capital to make the guaranteed payment. Enron would then have to reverse the profit and record a loss of $290 million. The large loss would further depress the Enron stock. Even with this risk, Enron created LJM and completed the deal. Enron considered LJM a large success and entered into similar arrangements to hedge other risky tech stock holdings. They called these arrangements Raptor partnerships.

The myriad of partnerships created was actually a sophisticated Ponzi scheme. Enron dealt with nearly 700 SPEs in all. Enron created fictitious profits to meet earnings expectations. Those profits would have to be offset in the future as losses. As the losses came due, Enron continued the process and created new structured deals to hide (or delay) the losses and generate additional profits. In this way the deals quickly mushroomed in number and in size. Eventually the scheme collapsed when Enron's stock price fell in 2001. Many of the partnerships funded with the stock were unable to complete their transactions. Enron was forced to disclose $1 billion in losses that it had previously booked as profits and was forced into bankruptcy.

Investment banks have denied any wrongdoing, saying they are

(*Continued*)

(*Continued*)

not responsible for Enron (or any other firm) fraudulently booking loans as revenue. However, the banks probably suspected that Enron's financial statements were misleading—at the very least. Even if the banks did nothing illegal, they violated the trust of its clients and public investors by participating in a scheme designed to hide a firm's financial troubles. The institutions failed in their corporate governance role as a monitor. This failure is particularly concerning because Morgan and Citigroup (the two largest players in the Enron fiasco) are the nation's two largest financial institutions.

While the Enron example details the role of investment banks in Enron's structured deals, evidence exists that banks have helped other firms create questionable SPEs. During the early 2000s, JP Morgan pitched these financing vehicles to other firms and entered into arrangements with seven companies. Citigroup discussed structured deals with 14 companies and developed them with 3.[7] Deals have also been structured by the bankers of Credit Suisse Group, Barclays PLC, FleetBoston Financial Corporation, Royal Bank of Scotland Group PLC, and Toronto-Dominion Bank.

SECURITIES ANALYSTS

Analysts generally fall into two categories: buy-side and sell-side. Institutional investors, such as pension funds and mutual funds, hire analysts. Their purpose is to help decide which stocks the fund should buy; therefore they are referred to as **buy-side analysts**. The recommendations of these analysts are not public and they are only seen and used by the institutional investors. Fund managers are managing money on behalf of individual investors, such as retirement accounts, so they are an important part of the corporate monitoring system (more on institutional investors in Chapter 7). Alternatively, brokerage and investment banks also employ analysts. These analysts hope that their research will generate enough interest in a security that their firm will generate trading commissions or underwriting business. As such, brokerage and investment bank analysts are commonly known as **sell-side analysts** and they often appear to act like salespeople for the stocks that they cover. The recommendations of sell-side analysts are commonly made public. Many investors rely on these recommendations and therefore sell-side analysts are also part of the corporate monitoring system. Our focus here will be on sell-side analysts.

To do his job, a sell-side analyst will look at a firm's operating and financial conditions, the firm's immediate and long-term future prospects, the effectiveness of its management teams, and the general outlook of the industry in which the firm belongs. Most analysts follow a specific industry to gain expertise in a particular sector. Based on their evaluations, analysts will make earnings predictions.

Usually they will try to predict the quarterly earnings per share (EPS) numbers. These predictions are useful to investors who rely on these estimates to determine the health of the companies in which they may or may not own stock. For example, many investors use P/E ratios (the market price of a share of stock divided by its annual earnings per share) as an important gauge of a stock's attractiveness as an investment. Some investors like to examine forward-looking P/E ratios. That is, they use a P/E ratio for next year's estimated earnings. Therefore these earnings estimates are important and useful to investors.

Perhaps more important, the analyst also makes trading recommendations to investors. For example, an analyst may suggest buying or selling a particular stock. These recommendations usually boil down to one-word or two-word recommendations such as "hold" or "buy." Further, some recommendations are ambiguous, such as "accumulate," "market perform," and "neutral." Is an "accumulate" recommendation as strong as a "buy" recommendation? Does a "neutral" rating mean "don't sell" and/or "don't buy?" Is a "market perform" rating good or bad? However, while we still see these kinds of recommendations today, there has been a trend toward making analysts' ratings less complicated and vague. Analysts at Goldman Sachs, Lehman Brothers, Merrill Lynch, Morgan Stanley, Prudential and other places are now using a three-tier rating system (buy, hold, and sell) to eliminate the ambiguity between ratings.[8]

Analyst recommendations should be timely. For example, if on a particular day an interested investor finds that the analyst's recommendation for a given stock is a buy, then that recommendation should reflect the analyst's most recent opinion. This means the recommendation should be updated frequently. If a news item breaks that could potentially affect an analyst's recommendation, then a revised and updated recommendation should be disseminated immediately. For her or his largest customers, the analyst may even make a phone call. However, a recommendation revision may sometimes have to go through an approval process, which may take a couple of days. Lengthy research reports that are mailed out or personally presented to potential investors may be a bit less timely as well. Nonetheless, investors generally rely on analysts for timely advice.

Quality of Analysts' Recommendations

The traditional roles of the analysts are to conduct thorough analyses of their assigned firms in order to make earnings estimates and to make trading recommendations. Further, they should also make timely stock recommendations. Are analysts good at these functions?

With regard to predicting earnings, analysts have consistently been slightly conservative. That is, analysts make earnings predictions that end up being slightly lower than the eventual actual earnings. This result may seem odd, especially given their known penchant for being overly optimistic. These "conservative" earnings predictions are well-known phenomena and involve two factors. First, companies like to meet or beat earnings expectations. Management will then be viewed as being good at their jobs and the company will be viewed as being as good as, or better than, expected.

Second, for analysts to do a good job at predicting earnings, they need information. If analysts have full access to the firms that they follow, such as personal meetings with the CEO or other top executives, then their task becomes easier. Will a CEO be 100 percent cooperative with an analyst who sets the estimate too high? Probably not. In fact, Bill Gates and sales chief Steve Ballmer of Microsoft once purposely criticized their own firm to analysts in order to depress their expectations. Later, on being told by one analyst that they had succeeded in painting a grim picture, Gates and Ballmer gave each other a high-five![9] This being the case, what is the general outcome of these two factors? Analysts make slightly conservative estimates because this is what management wants.[10] This result makes the CEO happy and willing to grant future access to the analyst. The analyst ends up being "off" on an estimate only by a very small margin and is still considered a good analyst. The company will either make or beat the estimate and it will be considered a good company. "Under promise, over deliver" is the name of this game.

The ability of analysts to predict earnings accurately may suffer in the future. Since October 2000, the SEC has prevented firms from divulging privileged information to any analyst. Information that the firm wishes to convey to an analyst must simultaneously be conveyed to the public. This new rule is known as **Regulation Fair Disclosure** or **Reg FD**. The SEC believes it unfair that some investors, through analysts, can gain private information that other investors cannot. The SEC policy creates a level playing field for all investors. For the analyst without privileged access to information, forecasting accuracy is likely to decline. However, forecasts now may possibly become more honest assessments of future earnings. The effect that this SEC regulation will have on analysts' forecasts cannot be predicted but one academic study finds that, since the SEC regulation was passed, forecasts have become less accurate.[11]

What about analysts' ability to recommend stocks? It is unclear whether analysts are good at picking stocks. Older academic studies from the 1970s contended that analysts did not have good stock-picking abilities. However, more recent studies suggest that analysts may have some marginal ability as stock pickers.[12] If you were to buy stocks recommended as a "strong buy" during 1985 to 1996 and hold them until the rating was downgraded, you would have out-performed the market by 4.3 percent per year, not considering transactions costs. Analysts did indeed pick good stocks. However, if transaction costs were considered, you would have under-performed the market by 3.6 percent. While the picks were good, they were not good enough to implement a successful trading strategy.

Perhaps even more revealing is the fact that during the early 2000s, only 2 percent of all stocks carried a sell recommendation,[13] despite the unambiguous bearishness of the markets at that time. Knowledgeable investors, however, know that a neutral or hold recommendation is really a sell signal. Nonetheless, the optimistic phrases used by analysts still promote a bullish attitude and not all investors are knowledgeable.

POTENTIAL CONFLICTS OF INTEREST

Analysts and the Firms They Analyze

Analysts want access to high quality information. Analysts may be better than the rest of us at assessing the quality of a firm but they also want to be better than the next analyst. To do this analysts will try to obtain as much information as possible. Of course the best source of a firm's information is the firm itself and analysts want to be able to have frank discussions with the firm's management. This situation represents an obvious conflict of interest. How can an analyst who needs access to management turn around and give the firm a bad rating? Would the analyst be able to gain access again?[14] Therefore analysts may have their hands tied. They may want to be objective but their objectivity may prevent them from getting access in the future.

In addition, because analysts typically specialize in a particular industry or two, they get to know the managers in those industries. They may even develop friendships with them. Specializing in a particular industry or sector allows the analyst to become an expert in the different influences and nuances of the industry. However, human nature tends to be optimistic and the circumstance where analysts are friends with the firm's management makes being objective difficult.

Analysts Working at Investment Banks

Analysts can work for an independent research firm, for a brokerage firm, or for the brokerage operation of an investment bank. Most high-profile analysts work for investment banks.

Consider that investment banks have corporate clients that are also firms that their analysts follow. The fees for investment banking services can easily run into the tens of millions of dollars. Will these analysts feel free to make public honest assessments if it would jeopardize those banking fees? If an analyst came out with a negative rating for a stock that his colleagues at the bank had underwritten earlier, then would not the bankers be upset? In addition, if a non-client firm received a negative assessment from an analyst, that firm might not give the analyst's firm any investment banking business. Analysts and investment bankers at the same bank are not supposed to collude or even influence each other when they are evaluating the same firm. This supposed separation between analysts and bankers within the bank is commonly referred to as a "Chinese Wall." However, analysts that work at investment banks may feel the need to compromise their integrity for the good of their employer.

Academic studies provide evidence consistent with this problem.[15] They find that stocks recommended by analysts who work at investment banks under perform stocks recommended by independent analysts. Also, according to a commentary in *Business Week*, the stock-picking performance of independent analyst firms, such as Callard Asset Management and Alpha Equity Research, out-performed the stock-picking performance of powerhouse investment banks, such as Goldman Sachs, Solomon Smith Barney, Morgan Stanley, and Merrill Lynch.[16] This evidence suggests that conflicts of interest faced by analysts at investment banks may compromise some of their recommendations.

In the late 1990s, analysts more commonly became a part of the investment banking team. When bankers were pitching their services to a firm who wanted to issue securities, an analyst would be there. After the bankers were hired to underwrite the security, they took the analyst on the road show to help market the issue to institutional investors. In this capacity, analysts become salespeople and promoters of the firm instead of objective analyzers of financial performance. As a result, a part of analysts' compensation has increasingly been dependent on the investment banking business that they can bring to the institution. For example, some star analysts have been receiving 75 percent of their compensation from the investment-banking side of the firm. As such, equity research departments were starting to seem like a support function for investment banking. This trend bucks the traditional view of what analysts do for a living. This partnership between traditionally separate arms of an investing banking firm leads to a serious conflict of interest problem.

EXAMPLE 5.3

MERRILL LYNCH: ANALYSTS VERSUS INVESTMENT BANKING

Merrill Lynch has been criticized for two apparent conflicts between analysts and investment banking in which the firm took the side of the bankers. The charge is that an analyst with a bearish recommendation on a firm was replaced with another analyst who was bullish to obtain investment banking business from the firm. Specifically, a more optimistic analyst replaced the previous analyst covering Enron in order to gain favor with Enron executives. Early in 1998, analyst John Olson recommended Enron stock with a "neutral" rating. Olson's negative rating and his personal style rubbed Enron executives Jeffrey Skilling and Ken Lay the wrong way. Merrill Lynch bankers complained to their CEO about not gaining any investment banking business with Enron while Olson rated the firm so poorly. The investment banking business kept going to banks where the analysts rated Enron as a "buy" or

better. In August 1998, Olson left Merrill for another company. Merrill then hired Donato Eassey to be the analyst covering Enron. Eassey quickly upgraded Enron to "accumulate." By the end of 1998, Merrill was providing investment banking services to Enron that would generate $45 million in fees.[17]

In another situation in 1999, Merrill replaced analyst Jeanne Terrile, who covered Tyco International, after Tyco CEO Dennis Kozlowski complained to Merrill CEO David Komansky.[18] The new analyst, Phua Young, promptly upgraded Tyco to a "buy" rating. The next year, Merrill underwrote Tyco's $3 billion stock issue. Both examples illustrate the strong power that public companies have over analysts who work at investment banks and the motivation of banks to be optimistic in order to gain underwriting business.

New Regulations

The days of analysts aspiring for a piece of the investment banking action may be over. Under the impetus of the Sarbanes-Oxley Act, the National Association of Securities Dealers (NASD rule 2711) and the NYSE (rule 472) both put forth new or amended rules that would address the conflict of interest problem in analyst research and opinion. The SEC approved these new regulations in the summer of 2002. Under the new rules, sell-side research analysts

1. cannot be subject to supervision from investment banking operations;
2. cannot have their compensation tied to investment banking deals; and
3. they cannot promise favorable ratings to lure investment-banking deals.

In addition, when an analyst provides research opinion, she must disclose

1. whether she received compensation based on investment banking revenue;
2. whether she holds a position as officer or director in the subject company; or
3. whether the subject company is a client of the firm.

To resolve SEC allegations of analyst misconduct, Merrill Lynch and nine other investment banking firms[19] settled with the SEC in 2003 and paid a combined $1.4 billion in fines and penalties. They also agreed to new analyst recommendation procedures (including following the new NASD and NYSE rules).[20] This settlement is known as the "Global Analyst Research Settlement." The Settlement between the Wall Street firms, the SEC, NASD, and the NYSE closely mirrors the NASD and NYSE new rules. However, it also mandates some additional rules, such as requiring banking and research departments to be physically separated and that the research department have a dedicated legal department. Also when giving analyst opinion on security issues, the investment bank must also offer at least one independent research "buy," "sell," or "hold" rating alongside their own analysts' ratings.

Have these new rules changed the analyst rating's bias? A recent study investigates this question. The authors examine the number of buy, hold, and sell ratings given by analysts during the approximately two years before and two years after the Settlement.[21] Notice from Panel A of Figure 5.2 that before the new rules, analysts rated 60.7 percent of the firms a "buy." Only 4.2 percent were rated a "sell." After the new regulations, analysts recommended 42.9 percent of rated firms a "buy" and 11.7 percent a "sell." It appears that the new rules have reduced the rating's bias. However, there still appears to be some over optimism.

Panels B and C focus on just those firms that are issuing equity (IPO or SEO). Some of the worst analyst bias appeared in investment banking firm affiliated analysts touting firms in which the bank was seeking as a client. Panel B shows that nearly 70 percent of these firms were given "buy" ratings and only 2.1 percent were given "sell" ratings. This optimism has weakened somewhat since the new regulations. After the new rules, 49 percent of issuing firms were given a "buy" rating by affiliated analysts and 6.5 percent were given "sell" ratings. Compare these rating's percentages with those given by analysts not affiliated with an investment bank reported in Panel C. Unaffiliated analysts were also optimistic before the rule change, giving a buy rating to 63.9 percent of the

PANEL A   ALL RATINGS

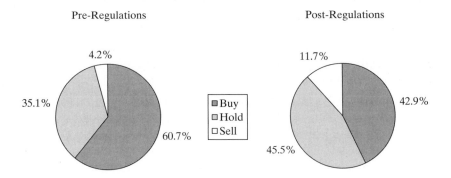

PANEL B   RATINGS ON FIRMS ISSUING EQUITY BY BANKING AFFILIATED ANALYSTS

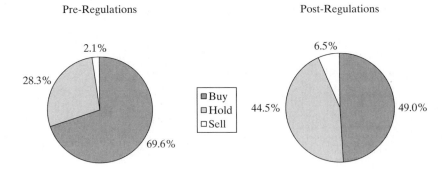

PANEL C   RATINGS ON FIRMS ISSUING EQUITY BY UNAFFILIATED ANALYSTS

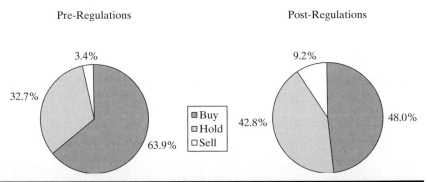

FIGURE 5.2   Distribution of Analyst Recommendations Before and After the Rule Changes

firms issuing capital. This changed to 48.0 percent after the rule change. Overall it appears that the NASD and NYSE rule changes along with the Settlement have reduced the analyst ratings bias.

Summary

Investment banks play a vital role in the American corporate system: They help firms acquire the capital they need to expand business operations. In order to underwrite the securities that firms' issue, the banks become intimately familiar with the operations of those firms. This situation gives them a unique ability to be corporate governance monitors. Capital is a scarce commodity and investment banks should be the gatekeepers and ensure that deserving companies obtain needed capital. This way they would bring only high quality firms and security issues to the public. During the internet craze, the banks failed in this role.

Analysts evaluate a firm's performance and future prospects and then make trading recommendations. For the most part, they generally seem good at it. However, two conflicts of interests in the system may compromise their objectivity at times. First, analysts want to gather good information through access to the management team of the firm, which requires a good relationship. This might be difficult to do when the analyst thinks the firm's prospects are poor. Second, analysts have been rewarded for luring investment-banking business to their employer. Consequently they were encouraged to be bullish on the firms they follow to keep both potential and current investment banking clients happy. Rules aimed at limiting these conflicts of interest have been passed. The SEC has also mandated that analysts certify that the opinions they express reflect their personal views. Some of these rules already seem to be working.

WEB Info about Investment Banks and Analysts

CFA Institute

www.cfainstitute.org

SEC Securities Analysts page

www.sec.gov/divisions/marketreg/securitiesanalysts.htm.com

Review Questions

1. What are the main ways an investment bank offers a security for sale?
2. Discuss why and how investment banks can be considered potentially effective monitors of corporations.
3. Why does it seem like IPOs are underpriced in the offering?
4. Describe how investment banks contributed to the investor confidence crisis in the early 2000s.
5. What is the financial analyst's function? How might analysts be important participants in the monitoring of the firm?
6. Are analysts good at evaluating firms? Elaborate.
7. Name and describe the conflicts of interest analysts face.

Discussion Questions

1. Provide some ideas on how investment banks can be made more conservative with regard to taking firms public.
2. When investment banks take firms public, they have in effect two clients: the going-public firm and the investors who buy the new shares. Which client do you think the bank is mostly concerned with? Why might they be equally concerned with both?
3. How would you standardize anlaysts' recommendations?
4. Some people think that fewer recommendations, such as simply recommending buy, hold, or sell, is the best system. What do think is the rationale behind this view? Do you agree?
5. What is your overall view of the sell-side analysts profession? Given that the accuracy of their recommendations does not directly lead profits for the analysts firm, how do you think sell-side analysts should be compensated?

Exercises

1. Find a firm that recently conducted an IPO. What are the details of the offering? Which investment bank(s) underwrote the offering? How successful was the offering from the perspectives of the firm, the banks, and investors? Do you think the firm was ready to conduct an IPO? Explain.
2. Find a firm that is scheduled to conduct an IPO in the near future. What types of information are provided to the interested investor? Describe how the information is useful in making a buy versus no-buy decision.
3. Provide a status report on the current state of investment banking. Are they underwriting fewer IPOs and SEOs? If so, then are they in danger of getting into financial trouble?
4. Go to the AIMR web site (*www.aimr.org*). Identify and describe the ideas that AIMR proposes to improve investor confidence in analyst recommendations. Evaluate the potential of these ideas for resolving the problems.
5. Describe the actions of Jack Grubman, former analyst for Salomon Smith Barney, Mary Meeker, the internet analyst at Morgan Stanley, and Henry Blodgett, former analyst at Merrill Lynch, that has led many to criticize analysts.
6. Pick a company and report its analysts' recommendations for trading and their predictions of future earning. Pick another company in the same industry and do the same. Does one company have a wider dispersion of analysts' recommendations and predictions? Why do you think this is?

Exercises for Non-U.S. Students

1. Describe the investment banking businesss in your country. Do you think they do a good job of bringing only good firms public? Explain your opinion.
2. Describe the nature of analysts in your country. Are securities analysts important in your country? How are they compensated?
3. To what extent are the problems outlined in this chapter pertinent to your country? Explain.

Endnotes

1. Jay Ritter and Ivo Welch, "A Review of IPO Activity, Pricing, and Allocations," *Journal of Finance* 57, no. 4 (2002): 1795–1828, and updated data available on Jay Ritter's website (*http://bear.cba.ufl.edu/ritter/*).

2. Alexander Ljungqvist and William Wilhelm, "IPO Allocations: Discriminatory or Discretionary?" *Journal of Financial Economics* 65, no. 2 (2002): 167–201.

3. Andrew Ross Sorkin, "Just Who Brought Those Duds to Market?" *New York Times,* April 15, 2001, 3.1.

4. Peter Elstrom, "The Great Internet Money Game," *Business Week* (April 26, 2001): 16.

5. Peter Fusaro and Ross Miller, *What Went Wrong at Enron* (Hoboken, NJ: John Wiley and Sons, 2002).

6. Peter Behr and April Witt, "Visionary's Dream Led to Risky Business," *Washington Post*, July 28, 2002, A1.

7. Jathon Sapsford and Paul Beckett, "Citigroup, J.P. Morgan Marketed Enron-Type Deals to Other Firms," *Wall Street Journal,* July 23, 2002, C13.

8. Stephanie Smith, "How are Analysts Changing?" *Money* (September 2002): 89.

9. Justin Fox, "Learn to Manage Your Earnings and Wall Street Will Love You," *Fortune* (March 31, 1997): 77–80.

10. Many academic articles have cited this phenomenon. For example, see Francois Degeorge, Jayendu Patel, and Richard J. Zeckhauser, "Earnings Management to Exceed Thresholds," *Journal of Business* 72 (1999).

11. Anup Agrawal, Sahiba Chadha, and Mark Chen, "Who Is Afraid of Reg FD? The Behavior and Performance of Sell-Side Analysts Following the SEC's Fair Disclosure Rules," to be published in the *Journal of Business*.

12. Brad Barber, Reuven Lehavey, Maureen McNichols, and Brett Trueman, "Can Investors Profit from the Prophets? Security Analyst Recommendations and Stock Returns," *Journal of Finance* 56 (2001): 531–563.

13. Marcia Vickers and Mike France, "How Corrupt Is Wall Street?" *Business Week* (May 13, 2002): 37–42.

14. One analyst said that without access, it becomes difficult to make quality stock assessments, akin to playing basketball with one hand tied behind your back (Marcia Vickers and Mike France, "How Corrupt Is Wall Street?" *Business Week* (May 13, 2002): 37–42).

15. Roni Michaely and Kent L. Womack, "Conflict of Interest and the Credibility of Underwriter Analyst Recommendations," *Review of Financial Studies* 12 (1999): 653–686. Brad Barber, Reuven Lehavy, and Brett Trueman, "Comparing the Stock Recommendation Performance of Investment Banks and Independent Research Firms," unpublished working paper at the University of Michigan.

16. Emily Thornton, "Research Should Pay Its Own Way," *Business Week* (June 3, 2002): 72.

17. Olson, Eassey, and Merrill Lynch all deny that anything inappropriate occurred. Indeed, Eassey was one of the few analysts to downgrade Enron when its troubles began to become public. See Richard Oppel, "Merrill Replaced Research Analyst Who Upset Enron," *New York Times,* July 30, 2002, 1.1.

18. Charles Gasparino, "Merrill Replaced Its Tyco Analyst After Meeting," *Wall Street Journal,* September 17, 2002, C1.

19. The firms were Citigroup Inc.; Credit Suisse First Boston Corp.; Morgan Stanley; Goldman Sachs Group Inc.; Lehman Brothers Holdings Inc.; Bear Stearns Cos.; U.S. Bancorp Piper Jaffray, a unit of U.S. Bancorp; J.P Morgan Chase & Co.; UBS AG and Merrill Lynch & Co. Former Merrill analyst Henry Blodget and former Citigroup analyst Jack Grubman also reached settlements with the SEC.

20. Colleen DeBaise, "Analyst Research Settlement With SEC Gets Final Approval," *Wall Street Journal* (November 3, 2003): C.12.

21. The data is from Ohad Kadan, Leonardo Madureira, Rong Wang, and Tzachi Zach, "Conflicts of Interest and Stock Recommendations: The Effects of the Global Settlement and Recent Regulations," Washington University working paper (July 2005).

6

CREDITORS AND CREDIT RATING AGENCIES

So far we have discussed corporate governance as if only stockholders should care about it. However, those who lend money to the firm (i.e. creditors) are also important investors to that firm. Therefore, lenders care about corporate governance too. In general, there are two kinds of lenders, institutional lenders such as a commercial bank and individual investors such as a bondholder.

Creditors can trade their claims just as stockholders can. For example, bondholders can sell their bonds to other investors (and banks can sell their loans too but primarily to other institutions). If firms suffer from poor corporate governance, then the value of their bonds might decline just like the value of the stock. If a firm collapses from poor corporate governance then lenders may get back only pennies on the dollar of their loan.

While a bank may find it worthwhile to monitor the firm that they lend to (because millions, even billions, could be at stake), individual bondholders may not have the resources to do so. Fortunately debt, in and of itself, could be a governance mechanism (we will explain this in more detail soon). Further, there are also credit rating agencies that rate the safety level of corporate debt. As such they can provide important information to potential bond investors. Therefore the existence of corporate debt creates three important corporate system monitors or devices:

1. monitoring by institutional lenders;
2. debt, in and of itself, can be a disciplinary mechanism; and
3. monitoring and debt ratings by credit agencies.

DEBT AS A DISCIPLINARY MECHANISM

When a firm has debt, it usually has to make promised interest payments every year. If the firm misses an interest payment, the lender can sue for control of the firm. On the other hand, if the firm's stockholders are not promised anything and though a firm can pay a dividend to its stockholders at the discretion of its board of directors, it is not legally obligated to do so. Because interest payments represent fixed annual obligations of the firm, debt actually imposes discipline on to the firm's management. That is, the firm's management has to generate enough revenue each year to cover the firm's interest expense. If the managers fail to do this, then they could lose control of the firm to a creditor.

While interest expense represents an important revenue hurdle that managers have to overcome and is thus a potentially effective motivator for management, it also discourages superfluous spending by management. That is, it limits managerial discretion. Of course, having to make large annual interest payments can also restrict a manager's flexibility to make value-enhancing capital expenditures when opportunities "suddenly" arise. Therefore, the use of debt to discipline firms may be limited primarily to mature firms.

Finally, in addition to a promised interest payment, other explicit **covenants** (these are rules, promises, and/or restrictions that the borrower agrees to legally adhere to) can be written into the debt contracts, such as guarantees by the borrower to protect its collateral value. The breaking of any covenant can transfer control of the firm from management to creditors. Because creditor rights are usually more explicit than shareholder rights, debt potentially provides better protection to investors than equity.[1]

EXAMPLE 6.1

DO FIRMS HAVE ENOUGH DEBT?

Some firms have significantly more annual earnings than annual interest expense. A times-interest-earned (TIE) ratio is usually measured as earnings before interest and taxes (EBIT) divided by total interest expense. For example, the TIE ratio for IBM is over 80. That is, IBM can pay its annual interest expense more than 80 times over. On the one hand, a high TIE ratio seems great but on the other hand, it could signal that the firm has low capital investment expenses for future growth opportunities. This latter scenario is not necessarily bad because firms eventually enter a maturity stage in their life-cycle but if the firm is not paying dividends (or enough dividends) then the firm could be retaining and holding on to too much cash. Cash is not the most productive asset and sometimes cash can be spent on bad projects just to get rid of it. This is not good for shareholders. One remedy for this problem would be to use excess cash to repurchase stock or raise dividends and then to borrow funds to finance its projects. The increase in interest expense may lead to a reduction in net income but with fewer shares outstanding the net income per share could be higher as a result of this capital structure change. In addition, because debt has a tax advantage as interest is paid before taxes, increases in debt, in and of itself, should increase the value of the firm. IBM has a TIE ratio of over 80 but less than 15 percent of their total assets are financed with long-term debt and meanwhile, it holds billions in cash and cash equivalents. After much criticism from investors and shareholders, at the end of 2004, Microsoft paid a special dividend of $3 per share, reducing its cash position by $32 billion.

INSTITUTIONAL LENDERS AS CORPORATE MONITORS

Banks will of course monitor firms that they lend to. Sometimes a firm will develop a long-term relationship with a bank. Relationship banking might be beneficial to the borrowing firm on at least two counts. First, the firm might be able to get a favorable interest rate from its bank. Second, the firm may feel it will be easier to renegotiate debt contracts (if necessary) with a single lender (i.e. the bank) than with disperse lenders (i.e. bondholders).

However, getting favorable interest rates from banks often entails the firm having to expose private information to the bank. For example, a firm may wish to borrow billions of dollars to embark on a new project. The firm could issue *public* debt (i.e. bonds) but may find that the interest rate (i.e. coupon rate) is too high for one reason or another (e.g. the firm could already have a lot of debt, the firm could have little collateral assets, etc.). This firm could opt to borrow from a bank or insurance company but to get a favorable rate it may have to reveal intimate details of its project to prove that it is worthy of a low interest rate. Further, the firm may have to agree to numerous covenants to get the favorable bank rate. As a single lender, it is easy for a bank to enforce covenants. Therefore the bank may end up having too much power over its borrowers.[2]

Why Didn't Lenders Raise a Red Flag During the Recent Corporate Scandals?

A firm's creditors and stock holders are often *both* viewed as investors but in reality creditors are literally lending to stockholders, thus putting these two investors on opposite sides of the credit claim. Therefore, these two investors do not necessarily share the same objectives for the firm.

From the balance sheet, note that stockholders are entitled to the firm's net income *after* creditors get their interest payment. That is, creditor's claims have seniority over equity holder's claims. This by itself can cause divergent incentives between the two claimants. Say, for example, the firm has to choose between a risky project with an uncertain high payoff and a safe project with a more certain marginal payoff. The return on the safe project may barely leave anything left over to stockholders once creditors are paid. Therefore stockholders may favor the risky project over the safe one but creditors might be indifferent between the two projects if both of them can cover the firm's interest expense. Because creditors get their returns first, they may have less incentive to monitor managerial behavior than stockholders.

Of course there is the possibility that managerial risk-taking may be so excessive that interest payments and principle repayment cannot be made but under these extreme circumstances, creditors can then force the firm to liquidate its assets to recover at least some of their investment claim.

Because debt claims are senior, both to the revenue and to the liquidation value, creditors may be less active in monitoring than stockholders.

CREDIT RATING AGENCIES

Just as analysts help rate stocks for potential stock investors, credit rating agencies rate bonds for potential bond investors. However, because bond investors are primarily risk-averse investors, they primarily care about the risk of the bond, which is the focus of these credit rating agencies.

The safety level of a bond is very important to those who choose fixed-income investments. The best return a bondholder can receive is both interest payments during the term of the bond and the principal upon maturity of the bond. Therefore bondholders focus on safety. How do you know if a firm's debt is safe or risky? Corporate bonds are given a safety rating. At least one of five firms—Moody's Investors Service, Standard & Poor's, Dominion Bond Rating Service, Fitch, and the new A.M. Best Co.—conducts a credit analysis and gives the firm a grade. This grade informs investors about the risk of a bond.

A Brief Historical Perspective

A brief history will help the understanding of how the credit industry works and of its importance. John Moody invented credit ratings in 1909 when he published a manual of ratings on 200 railroads and their securities.[3] He made his money by charging investors for the manual. By 1916, The Standard Company, the predecessor to Standard & Poor's, started rating bonds and Fitch started rating bonds in 1920. By the 1970s, photocopy equipment was so prevalent that many investors obtained ratings without paying for the published books. However, the demand for the ratings was so great that rating companies could give the ratings free to investors and still earn money by charging the bond issuers fees to rate their bonds.

After the stock market crash of 1929 and the Great Depression, the government looked for ways to restore confidence in the banking system. The securities acts of 1933 and 1934 went a long way toward increasing regulation of the banking and securities industries. However, in 1936, the government expanded the role of credit ratings by requiring that commercial banks only hold high quality debt. Specifically, the Comptroller of the Currency decreed that banks could only own "investment-grade" bonds; this and other categories of ratings are illustrated in the next section. Because one large and influential type of investor (commercial banks) needed credit ratings on debt instruments in order to buy them, all bond issuers wanted to be rated. Today, anyone who wants to issue bonds in the

U.S. needs to be rated. This applies to companies, state and local governments, and even foreign governments.

While the credit rating helps investors understand the riskiness of a bond issue, the company pays the bill. In other words, a company planning a bond issue could discuss it with several credit agencies and see which one would give them the highest grade. A high quality rating for a company means that they can offer bonds at a low interest rate and still easily sell them all. A lower quality rating would require offering the bonds at a higher interest rate and it would cost the firm millions of dollars more in interest payments. Unscrupulous rating agencies could sell high ratings to firms willing to pay higher fees for them. In the wake of the 1975 scandalous bond default of Penn Central Corporation, the SEC designated three ratings agencies as the only ones satisfying rating regulations. The three anointed agencies, called **Nationally Recognized Statistical Rating Organizations (NRSROs)**, were Moody's, Standard & Poor's, and Fitch. The SEC later designated four more agencies as valid but mergers between the firms left only the three original firms. In February 2003, the SEC approved a fourth firm, Dominion Bond Rating Service (of Canada). In March 2005, the SEC approved a fifth firm, A.M. Best Co. Nevertheless, Moody's and Standard & Poor's have 80 percent of the market share and this is an uncompetitive environment for the industry.

The situation of a small number of firms in an industry is called an oligopoly. The SEC rules protect the five firms from further competition by preventing any other firms from joining the industry. Other small credit agencies exist but they must survive on the fees investors will pay for the evaluations. Finding substantial subscribers is difficult when the NRSROs provide free ratings. The SEC wants to give the designation to agencies that have large staffs and resources. Small credit rating agencies have tried and failed to obtain the SEC designation. These undesignated small agencies find themselves in a catch-22 position. These firms cannot get the SEC designation until they are larger but they cannot afford to grow without the fees they could charge with the designation.

With a lack of competition by new entrants, the five credit rating agencies operate very profitable businesses. The credit analysis process does not require expensive factories or machine tools. Low expenses and the low level of competition lead to high profits. Moody's profit margin is estimated to be 50 percent while Standard & Poor's is closer to 30 percent. These five firms have been immensely rewarded in the protected environment.

The Ratings

To assess the credit worthiness of companies, the credit agencies employ financial analysts who examine the firms' financial positions, business plans, and strategies. This means that the analysts carefully review public financial statements issued by the companies. To assist in their investigations, the SEC has granted the agencies an exemption from disclosure rules so that companies can reveal non-public or sensitive information to the agencies in confidence. Companies have no obligation to reveal special information but they often do so to convince the agencies that their debt issues should be rated highly. Credit analysts can often question CEOs and other top executives directly when conducting reviews because of the importance of credit ratings.

The rating systems of Moody's and Standard & Poor's are shown in Example 6.2. Notice that the two ratings agencies have similar systems.[4] Also both agencies can partition the ratings further. Moody's includes 1, 2, or 3 after the rating to show that the firm falls near the bottom, middle, or top of the scale within the category. Standard & Poor's uses a minus $(-)$ or plus $(+)$ sign. Consider two companies that want to borrow $1 billion by issuing bonds. The rating company rates the first company in the "high quality" category. This firm will have to pay 6.9 percent (or $69 million) in interest every year. The second firm is rated "non-investment grade" and would have to pay $99 million annually. These amounts differ substantially. Riskier companies pay higher interest.

If a company becomes financially stronger over time, then the bond rating will also improve. Therefore, the interest rate demanded by investors will fall, as illustrated in Example 6.2. When interest rates fall, bond prices rise. Consequently, if a firm becomes safer, then the price of its bonds will increase, which is what bondholders want. Alternatively, if the firm becomes riskier, then bond prices fall. The worst-case scenario for a bondholder is for the issuing company to default on the bonds and file for bankruptcy protection. Bondholders typically receive only a small portion of their principal back if a firm defaults.

The ratings that credit agencies issue have historically been good predictors of the default potential of a debt issuer. Only 0.5 percent of firms rated at the highest level (best quality) default.[5] This percentage increases to only 1.3 percent for issuers rated as high quality. However, the increase in the default rate substantially

EXAMPLE 6.2

RATINGS OF BOND SAFETY AND EXAMPLE BOND YIELDS

	Moody's Rating	*Standard & Poor's Rating*	*Example Bond Yield, %*
Best Quality	Aaa	AAA	6.4
High Quality	Aa	AA	6.9
Upper Medium Grade	A	A	7.1
Medium Grade	Baa	BBB	7.8
Non-Investment Grade	Ba	BB	9.9
Highly Speculative	B	B	10.5
Defaulted or Close To It	Caa to C	CCC to D	20 to 90

increases to 19.5 percent in the non-investment-grade bonds and 54.4 percent in the CCC category.

When a firm begins to struggle financially, credit agencies downgrade the ratings on its securities. A bond issue rated AAA− might be downgraded to AA+ or even AA. If the business operations or cash position of the firm continues to decline, the rating could fall further. Each downgrade signals to investors that the bonds are becoming riskier. In response, the price of the bonds declines and investors experience a capital loss. The term "investment grade" in the regulations is interpreted as ratings of BBB− or higher. If a bond slips to BB+ or lower, it is not considered investment grade. In fact, the popular term for non-investment-grade bonds is junk bonds. For additional protection of a bondholder's principal, many modern debt offerings include a rule (or covenant) that requires the company to increase the interest payment made on the bonds if the rating slips to junk status. Some bond covenants require the company to pay back the principal if the rating slips to junk. While this sounds like a good idea for bond investors, in practice it often triggers the very bankruptcy filing that bondholders try to avoid. A firm's debt is downgraded to junk bond status because the company is having some financial difficulty. If the firm suddenly owes higher interest payments or even hundreds of millions of dollars in principal, it is pushed into a more financially precarious position. The very covenant rules that try to protect the interest of bondholders can actually drive a company toward insolvency.

Criticisms

One criticism of credit agencies is that they have started to enter the consulting business. Being both consultants and credit raters creates a conflict of interest similar to the one that occurred when auditing firms were also consultants for a company. If the credit agency is earning lucrative consulting fees, then it might not be able to provide unbiased analysis of the firm's financial position. Just as auditing firms should not be allowed to audit companies where they act as consultants, neither should credit agencies rate the debt securities of companies to which they provide consulting services.

A second criticism is that the credit agencies have been given the same First Amendment rights as the media. When disgruntled companies or investors have sued the credit agencies, the agencies have been successful in using the free speech protection as a defense. The combination of regulated protection from new competitors, exemptions from disclosure rules, and First Amendment protection in court, makes credit agencies nearly invincible. That is, market forces (such as competition) and the court system would have difficulty disciplining them.

While the total record of credit agencies is fairly accurate, they have made some dramatic mistakes. A questionable call by the credit agencies occurred with the issuance of WorldCom bonds in May 2001. WorldCom issued an American record $11.9 billion of bonds, of which $10.1 billion was new financing. Standard & Poor's rated WorldCom and the massive debt issue investment grade, with a BBB+; Moody's rated it A3.[6] The massive offering by WorldCom should have come with a robust analysis by the investment banks as the underwriters and by the credit rating agencies.

One year later, in May 2002, the credit agencies downgraded WorldCom debt to junk-bond status. The rationale behind the downgrade was that WorldCom's total debt of $30 billion was too high.[7] Why were the agencies unconcerned with the debt level the previous year when WorldCom increased its debt by 50 percent with the massive bond issue? The agencies' initial seal of approval on the giant bond issue and the company downgrade one year later based on that same issue seems hard to believe. The high rating by the agencies allowed WorldCom to borrow that much money in the first place. The next month, on June 25, 2002, WorldCom disclosed that it had improperly booked $3.8 billion as capital investments instead of operating expenses over the previous five quarters. It found several more billion in accounting fraud over the next couple of months.

Credit agencies are not blameless in the corporate scandals of 2001 and 2002. Indeed, their special relationships with companies allows them to obtain private information that other monitors, such as independent analysts, might not receive. Of the outside monitors, credit rating agencies might have been in the best position to detect corporate fraud and warn investors. Yet in some cases these groups were one of the last to respond.

EXAMPLE 6.3

ENRON'S CREDIT RATING

The price of a share of Enron stock was $90 in August 2000 but by April 2001 the stock price had fallen to $60 per share. In the late summer, the price continued to fall and reached less than $40 per share. Even in November 2001, just before Enron declared bankruptcy, the stock had declined to less than $5 per share. This decline in Enron's stock price should have been a huge warning that something was drastically amiss. As it turned out, the credit agencies might have been more enablers than watchdogs.

The investment banks had raised capital for Enron's offshore partnerships, which Enron used to falsify loans as profits. The banks had invested hundreds of millions of dollars of their own money in Enron and its associated partnerships. The banks knew that if Enron filed for bankruptcy protection, their losses would be enormous. The banks also knew that if the credit rating agencies were to downgrade Enron to non-investment grade status, at least $3.9 billion in debt repayment would immediately be required. Enron would be forced to declare itself insolvent.

On November 8, 2001, the news about the partnerships and the massive losses became public. The stock price went down to less than $10 per share. The banks needed to act quickly or take massive losses; they wanted the credit agencies to hold off on their downgrade while they looked for new capital with which to save Enron.

Apparently the credit agencies delayed in downgrading Enron to non-investment grade. At first they merely downgraded the firm to the lowest levels of investment-grade ratings. Because companies seek a rating on debt they issue and investment banks help them issue the debt securities, banks and credit agencies frequently work together. The bankers may have used this relationship to convince the credit agencies to give them some time to save Enron.

To locate a buyer, investment banks Merrill Lynch and J.P. Morgan looked across town from the headquarters of Enron and found Dynegy. Enron and Dynegy executives began merger negotiations in November 2001. If they could agree, Dynegy would infuse Enron with $1.5 billion of cash to tide them over until the final merger could take place. The credit rating agencies knew that if the merger did not take place, Enron would be in deep financial trouble.

Yet instead of communicating this enormous risk to bondholders via a downgrade to junk bond status, the agencies waited. Given what the agencies knew, this situation was a large gamble for bondholders, like flipping a coin. Heads the merger goes through and the financial situation improves, tails it does not and Enron probably goes into bankruptcy. Investors might take this risk in speculative stocks but not in investment-grade bonds. The stock price had fallen to less than $5 per share. The credit rating agencies failed to warn investors how risky the situation had become.

On November 26, the Enron merger with Dynegy was dead. Enron was still discovering how vast the partnership problems were becoming. The designated credit rating agencies downgraded Enron to junk bond status on November 28. Enron's stock price fell to $0.61 per share. On December 2, 2001, Enron filed for bankruptcy protection. Bondholders waited in line at bankruptcy court with other creditors and hoped to regain some of their principal.

When NRSRO-designated agencies do make mistakes, they often claim the company lied to them. However, the agency's job is to validate the information they receive and then make conclusions based on its own analysis. What purpose do agencies serve as independent monitors if they simply follow the lead of the company executives?

INTERNATIONAL PERSPECTIVE

Japan's Main Bank System

In most countries, bank debt is the primary form of corporate borrowing and even the primary source of new financing. Japan is an interesting case (and Germany is similar to the Japanese case in many respects). Most developing markets rely on bank debt due to the lack of a sophisticated public debt market but Japan is a developed market whose firms rely heavily on bank debt. Firms in Japan have built long-term relationships with banks, usually with each firm having a "main bank." These main banks usually own equity and place its own personnel into important management positions (including directorships) of the borrowing firms.

During the 1980s, the Japanese main bank system was viewed as an ideal corporate governance model. Such bank-reliant firms had few conflicts among creditors, large stockholders, and management, as they were all linked by a single entity, the main bank. Because the bank had dual stakes as both a creditor and equity holder, they were well-known as active monitors of the Japanese firm. As a result, these firms were able to maintain high debt levels and had little need to maintain liquid financial slack. That is, firms did not have to keep cash reserves because they were able to get cash quickly from their main bank whenever they needed it. Further, when these bank-reliant firms experienced financial difficulties, the main banks were able to bail them out before the problem became serious. Thus, banks were viewed as effective monitors of firms.

However, in 1990, the Japanese market crashed and Japan has been in a bear market ever since, thus raising some doubts as to the efficacy of the main bank system. What might be the flaws of having influential bank monitors? First, banks might encourage client firms to pursue profit stabilization rather than profit maximization, in order to protect their claims as the firms' largest creditors. That is, banks might have too much power over their client firms, where they influence the firm in the best interests of a creditor rather than as a stockholder. Second, and perhaps most importantly, when banks experience financial difficulties, as Japanese banks did during the 1990s, then their client firms will also suffer.[8]

Creditor Rights Around the World

Creditors may also be protected by the legal system. For example, do a country's laws make it easy or difficult for a creditor to seize the collateral of a loan when the firm goes into bankruptcy reorganization? Do firms need the permission of the creditors to reorganize? Example 6.4 shows the strength of creditors' rights in countries throughout the world.[9] The index can vary from 0 to 4 and was formed by determining whether the laws in the country has any of the following four creditor rights:

1. no automatic stay on the assets in reorganization;
2. secured creditors get paid first;
3. restrictions for going into reorganization; and
4. management is replaced in reorganization.

A Creditor Rights index value of 4 means the country strongly protects creditors.

The companies are categorized by the legal origin from which the laws have evolved. The English legal system is based on **common law**. French, German, and

EXAMPLE 6.4

CREDITOR RIGHTS AROUND THE WORLD

Country	Creditor Rights	Country	Creditor Rights
Australia	1	Argentina	1
Canada	1	Belgium	2
Hong Kong	4	Brazil	1
India	4	Chile	2
Ireland	1	Colombia	0
Israel	4	Ecuador	4
Kenya	4	Egypt	4
Malaysia	4	France	0
New Zealand	3	Greece	1
Nigeria	4	Indonesia	4
Pakistan	4	Italy	2
Singapore	4	Mexico	0
South Africa	3	Netherlands	2
Sri Lanka	3	Peru	0
Thailand	3	Philippines	0
United Kingdom	4	Portugal	1
United States	1	Spain	2
Zimbabwe	4	Turkey	2
English-origin average	**3.11**	Uruguay	2
		French-origin average	**1.58**
Austria	3		
Germany	3	Denmark	3
Japan	2	Finland	1
South Korea	3	Norway	2
Switzerland	1	Sweden	2
Taiwan	2	**Scandinavian-origin average**	**2.00**
German-origin average	**2.33**		

Scandinavian legal systems are based on **civil law**. Common law is formed by precedents and judges that resolve specific disputes. Civil law uses statutes, comprehensive codes, and legal scholars to organize and formulate rules. Example 6.4 shows there is considerable variation of creditor rights within each legal origin.

But on average, countries that have an English-origin legal system have stronger protections for creditors. This empowers creditors to monitor the firm.

Summary

When a company obtains capital through borrowing money, it also obtains another governance mechanism. The need to pay interest and principle payments disciplines executives to manage the cash flow of the firm carefully and discourages superfluous spending. Those institutions and investors who lend the firm money become another monitor of the firm. Large creditors, such as banks, insurance companies, mutual funds, and pension funds, often develop close relationships with firms and can be effective monitors. Individual investors tend to rely on the recommendations of credit rating agencies.

The credit agency's purpose is monitoring debt issuers to protect public investors. However, the industry's structure creates a situation in which the agencies interact only a little with the investors they are protecting. Instead debt issuers pay agencies to give a rating. Agencies work with the issuers and the investment bankers to obtain information about the debt issue. Most of their business relies on the interactions with corporate participants, not with investors. In this process they gain access to private information about the firm. Overall, the NRSRO-designated agencies have done a good job of showing bond investors the level of risk they take in various bond issues.

Most of the agencies' interactions and the fees they earn are with the firms they rate, not the investors who use the ratings. This circumstance can create misaligned incentives. In addition, the U.S. government has made credit rating a closed and non-competitive industry that seems to have unusual immunity under the First Amendment in the court system. This immunity prevents investors from seeking damages when the agencies make mistakes. The lack of disciplinary market and legal forces can make the agencies lax in their watchdog duties.

WEB Info about Credit Rating Agencies

SEC Division of Market Regulation: Credit Agencies
www.sec.gov/divisions/marketreg/ratingagency.htm

Standard & Poor's
www2.standardandpoors.com

Moody's
www.moodys.com

Review Questions

1. Describe how debt, in and of itself, might keep management in check?
2. Describe the efficacy of financial institutions to be corporate monitors.
3. How are credit rating agencies important for firms, investors, and investment banks?

4. Why is the distinction between investment grade and non-investment grade ratings so important?
5. The SEC awards the Nationally Recognized Statistical Rating Organization designation. What criteria do they use to give the designation?

6. How did the rating agencies fail Enron bondholders and creditors?
7. Name and describe the conflicts of interest that credit agencies face.

Discussion Questions

1. Debt financing has a tax-advantage that equity financing does not have. Given this fact, do you think large U.S. firms have enough debt? In your opinion, which kinds of firms might be able to handle more debt?
2. If you were a CEO of a small high-tech firm and you wanted to borrow money for your firm, would you borrow from an institution such as a bank or would you issue bonds? Why? What if you were the CEO of General Electric?

3. In the U.S. it is difficult for a bank to be a lender and a stockholder for legal reasons (refer to the Glass-Steagall Act). What do you think are the cost and benefits of preventing bank lenders from being stockholders?
4. There are only five NRSRO-designated rating firms. What might be done to increase the number of rating firms?

Exercises

1. This chapter mentioned IBM as a possible candidate to have more debt in its capital structure. Try to identify another firm and describe why it is an ideal candidate to have more debt.
2. Find two firms from the same industry, but with different debt ratios. Try to work out why the two firms have different debt ratios. Try to find another pair of firms that have different debt ratios, but for a reason other

than the ones that you cited for the first pair.
3. Try to identify a firm that has more bank debt than public debt and vice versa. Try to work out why each firm prefers its debt type.
4. Obtain the ratings from at least four credit rating firms for one company. Compare the ratings.
5. Obtain the credit ratings for a firm over the past five years. How and why has the rating changed?

Exercises for Non-U.S. Students

1. What is the primary source of financing for the firms in your country? Do you think this is best for the future financial development of your country? Explain.
2. Do you think banks have too much or too little power in your country's corporate landscape? Explain.
3. Compared to the firms in the U.S., do the firms in your country have more

or less debt in their capital structure? Why do you suppose this is? Do you think this is good or bad for your country's firms?
4. Does your country have credit rating agencies? If so, describe the system and compare them to the U.S. credit rating agency system.

Endnotes

1. There is large literature on how debt, in and of itself, can restrict managerial discretion and is thus a corporate governance device. Michael C. Jensen, "The Agency Costs of Free Cash Flow: Corporate Finance and Takeovers," *American Economic Review,* Vol. 76, No. 2 (May, 1986) is a representative and well-known academic paper on this topic.

2. Perhaps the best academic papers that discuss monitoring by lenders is Diamond, Douglas W., "Monitoring and Reputation: The Choice between Bank Loans and Directly Placed Debt," *Journal of Political Economy,* 1991, *99*(4), 689–721, Rajan, R., "Insiders and Outsiders: The Choice Between Relationship and Arm's Length Debt," *Journal of Finance,* 47, 1992, 1367–1400, and Sharpe, S., "Asymmetric Information, Bank Lending and Implicit Contracts: A Stylized Model of Customer Relationships," *Journal of Finance,* 45, 1990, 1069–1087.

3. Amy Borrus, Mike McNamee, and Heather Timmons, "The Credit-Raters: How They Work and How They Might Work Better," *Business Week* (April 8, 2002): 38.

4. Ratings categories are from *www.moodys.com* and *www.standardandpoors.com.*

5. Standard & Poor's estimates use data from 1987–2001.

6. "WorldCom Smashes Records with $11.9 bn Blowout Bond," *Euroweek,* May 11, 2001, 4.

7. Gregory Zuckerman and Shawn Young, "Leading the News: WorldCom Debt Is Slashed to 'Junk'," *Wall Street Journal,* May 10, 2002, A3.

8. Good academic articles about Japan's main bank system is Takeo Hoshi, Anil Kashyap, and David Scharfstein, "The Role of Banks in Reducing the Costs of Financial Distress in Japan, *Journal of Financial Economics* 27 (1990): 67–88, Michael S. Gibson, "Can Bank Health Affect Investment? Evidence from Japan," Journal of Business 68 (July 1995): 281–308, and David E. Weinstein and Yishay Yafeh," On the Cost of a Bank Centered Financial System: Evidence from the Changing Main Bank Relations in Japan, *Journal of Finance* 53 (1998): 635–672.

9. The creditor rights index values are obtained from Table 4 of Rafael LaPorta, Florencio Lopex-de-Silanes, and Andrei Shleifer, and Robert W. Vishny, "Law and Finance," *Journal of Political Economy* 106 (1998): 1113–1155.

7

SHAREHOLDERS AND SHAREHOLDER ACTIVISM

W hen corporate scandals occur, shareholders are often viewed as innocent and helpless victims. Investors may be categorized into two groups: individual investors, such as you, your parents, and Microsoft's Bill Gates, and institutional investors, such as pension funds, insurance companies, and mutual funds. Many institutional investors actually invest on behalf of many smaller individual investors. Shareholders, both individuals and institutions, lose money when corporate scandals occur and firms subsequently go bankrupt. Thus they have expressed a desire for more protection and monitoring of their firm. This very desire for more protection has everyone, from the stock exchanges to the SEC, trying to find ways to protect investors. However, one question that begs asking is why cannot shareholders also take care of themselves? That is, why do they not take more responsibility for the stocks that they own?

People who own homes will often take precautions to safeguard themselves against burglary. Various ways to protect a home range from forming neighborhood watches, buying a watchdog, or installing a security system, to simply locking the doors each night. Of course, homeowners also rely on the local police to protect their homes, much like investors might rely on the SEC to protect their investments, but the police obviously cannot guarantee that all homes will be perfectly protected. This is just as true with shareholders' stocks.

There are valid reasons why individual investors do not pay more attention to what they own. Most individual shareholders do not own enough stock in any one company to be able to influence its management. Nor do most shareholders think it worth their time and effort to do anything. The gains (e.g. stock price increases) from their efforts would be shared by all other shareholders, while they alone would bear the costs. If shareholders do anything at all, they sell shares that they are unhappy with, commonly known as doing the "Wall Street walk."

Institutional shareholders that own many different stocks have some restrictions about what they can own and, for them, exerting some of their ownership rights may be worthwhile. Further, given the large amounts of stocks that these shareholders own, they may be able to affect the decision-making of the firm. Also the potential benefits accrued from their activism may be large enough to be worth the effort. Perhaps institutional shareholders can do more, especially given the fact that individuals have entrusted them to invest their money. According to the Survey of Consumer Finances, the trend is for individuals to own stocks through a fund rather than own stocks directly. In 2001, for example, 69.9 percent of U.S. households invested through mutual funds or pension funds compared to 21.3 percent that owned stocks directly. This is an increase from 1989 when 44.3 percent of families owned a fund and 16.9 percent owned stocks directly. Therefore institutional share-holder activism could play an important role in monitoring management.

This chapter discusses investor activism of various forms, including ways that individual shareholders can exert some influence over the firms that they own. The focus, however, will be on activism by institutional shareholders. Problems and constraints that institutional shareholders currently face are also described.

WHAT IS SHAREHOLDER ACTIVISM?

There is no formal definition of shareholder activism. Loosely speaking, any time shareholders express their opinions to try to affect or to influence a firm they are being active shareholders. Shareholders who vote their shares submit proposals to be voted on or attend annual shareholder meetings could certainly be considered active. Even writing a letter to management regarding some aspect of the firm's operations or social policies could be considered investor activism. We discuss the activism by three kinds of shareholders: individual shareholers, large shareholders (defined as the owner of a large portion of a firm's shares), and institutional shareholders. Note that these shareholder types are not mutually exclusive. Either an individual or insitutional investor can be a large shareholder.

Activism by Individual Shareholders

An individual investor with only a modest number of shares is able to attend shareholder meetings, submit proposals to be voted by at those meetings and vote at those meetings. Lewis Gilbert is generally credited with being the first individ-ual shareholder activist.[1] In 1932, as the owner of 10 shares of New York's Consolidated Gas Company, he attended its annual meeting. While at the meeting, he was surprised and appalled that he was not given a chance to ask questions. After all, he was a part-owner (albeit a small one) of the firm. Subsequently, Gilbert and his brother pushed for reform and, in 1942, the SEC created a rule to allow shareholders to submit proposals that could be put to a vote.

Today, anyone owning more than $2,000 or 1 percent of a firm's stock on a continuous basis for at least one year is able to submit a proposal to be considered and voted on at a shareholders' meetings. Firms are supposed to solicit proposals prior to their shareholder meetings. About a thousand shareholder proposals are submitted each year. In the example below, we show Goodrich Corporation's call for shareholder proposals to be considered and voted on at its upcoming annual shareholders' meeting.

EXAMPLE 7.1

GOODRICH'S CALL FOR SHAREHOLDER PROPOSALS

Shareholder Proposals for 2006 Annual Meeting

Under Securities and Exchange Commission rules, if a shareholder wants us to include a proposal in our proxy statement for presentation at the 2006 Annual Meeting, the proposal must be received by us, attention: Office of the Secretary, at our principal executive offices by November 7, 2005. We suggest that such proposals be sent by certified mail, return receipt requested.

Under our By-Laws, the proposal of business that is appropriate to be considered by the shareholders may be made at an annual meeting of shareholders by any shareholder who was a shareholder of record at the time of giving the notice described below, who is entitled to vote at such meeting and who complies with the notice procedures set forth in the By-Laws.

For business to be properly brought before an annual meeting of shareholders, the shareholder must have given timely notice thereof in writing to our Secretary. To be timely, the shareholder's notice must have been sent to, and received by, our Secretary at our principal executive offices generally not less than 90 nor more than 120 days prior to the first anniversary of the preceding year's annual meeting. For the 2005 Annual Meeting such notice must have been received between December 27, 2004 and January 26, 2005 and for the 2006 Annual Meeting such notice must be received between December 9, 2005 and January 8, 2006. Each such notice must include:

- for each matter, a brief description thereof and the reasons for conducting such business at the annual meeting;
- the name and address of the shareholder proposing such business as well as any other shareholders believed to be supporting such proposal;
- the number of shares of each class of Goodrich stock owned by such shareholders; and
- any material interest of such shareholders in such proposal.

This notice requirement applies to matters being brought before the meeting for a vote. Shareholders, of course, may and are encouraged to ask appropriate questions at the meeting without having to comply with the notice provisions.

By Order of the Board of Directors

Sally L. Geib
Secretary

Source: 2005 Goodrich Proxy Statement, page 43, available at http://ir.goodrich.com

Today, most shareholder proposals are governance-oriented, primarily attempting to forge an alignment between shareholder views and managerial actions. For example, proposals may address issues related to anti-takeover amendments, shareholder voting rules, or board composition.[2] Having these proposals passed, or even brought to the attention of the managers, can certainly have a potentially positive effect on the firm.

Lee Greenwood is an active shareholder well-known to General Mills management. Greenwood once simply suggested that Wheaties® should appear

---

EXAMPLE 7.2

FICTITIOUS EXERPT OF NOTICE OF PRETEND COMPANY SHAREHOLDER MEETING

Item No. 4

Ms. Gwen Smith, 1234 Main St., South Park, MI 48199, owner of approximately 101 shares of common stock, has given notice that she intends to present for action at the annual meeting the following resolution:

> To be resolved: 'That the Board of Directors no longer issue executive stock options, nor allow any current stock options to be repriced or renewed.
>
> REASON: 'The firm appears to be issuing too many stock options. Instead, executives should be compensated with actual stock instead of options. Actual stock may better align management and shareholders. If you AGREE please mark your proxy FOR this resolution.' "

The Board of Directors recommends a vote AGAINST the adoption of this proposal for the following reasons:

Pretend Company has granted stock options for many years and believes it to be a useful incentive compensation tool.

Management endorses the granting of stock options as an incentive to generate long-term stock price appreciation. Eliminating executive options may impair the firm's ability to retain high quality executives and to achieve sustained future growth.

The Board of Directors recommends a vote AGAINST this stockholder proposal, Item No. 4. Proxies solicited by the Board of Directors will be so voted unless stockholders specify a different choice.

While some individual shareholders are active shareholders and thus submit proposals, most individual shareholders are passive and do not submit proposals. These inactive shareholders are reluctant to vote against the firm's management. Therefore, while we have a system in place that allows active individual shareholders to submit proposals, their proposals rarely pass, especially when they go against managements' desires.

on airlines and in hotels.[3] Among individual shareholder activists, Evelyn Y. Davis is perhaps the most well-known and has been featured in *People* magazine.[4] As the modest shareholder of about 120 firms, Davis attends about 40 shareholder meetings each year. What does she do at these meetings? As everyone from journalists to executives seems to put it, she "raises hell." Davis has berated executives for everything from questionable merger decisions to the enormous size of their pay. Most individual shareholder activists use less dramatic methods. However, enough people like Evelyn Davis vigorously and frequently make themselves heard to have been deemed "corporate gadflies."

In practice, however, most shareholder proposals submitted by individual investors do not pass, especially those that go against management desires and those that involve obtaining a board seat. One reason is that it is difficult and expensive for one shareholder to communicate with all other shareholders. While it is easy for management to express its opinions and recommendations on submitted proposals. Below, we show what a communication to shareholders from management might look like. The communication is a shareholder meeting announcement, and one of the items in the announcement is a description of a proposal to be voted on and the board's assessment of the proposal. Though it is a fictitious example, it is adapted from an actual shareholder meeting announcement.

EXAMPLE 7.3

INDIVIDUAL INVESTORS IN ACTION

During 2000, Computer Associates (CA) stock price had dropped from a $70 high in January to about $30 in September. In the following year, Sam Wyly sponsored a proposal to unseat four CA board members.[5] After a highly publicized and expensive campaign, Wyly's proposal was defeated, primarily because it also sought to unseat the firm's cofounder and board chairman, Charles Wang. This example does not mean, however, that proposals, and even defeats, are fruitless or that shareholders should give up. Robert A.G. Monks spent $250,000 to run for a board seat at Sears in 1991. His effort resulted in defeat but the publicity eventually caused Sears to make massive changes on its own.[6]

Proposals do sometimes gain majority support. John Chevedden sponsored a proposal in 2001 to change the way board members are elected at Airborne Freight and he gained the support of 71 percent of the voting shareholders.[7] During that same year, Guy Adams beat tremendous odds with his bid for a board seat. As the owner of 1,100 shares of Lone Star restaurant stock, or 0.005 percent of the company, he was disgruntled because his stock had plummeted in value

(Continued)

(*Continued*)

while the CEO's income rose. Consequently Adams ran for a board seat, one held by the restaurant CEO Jamie B. Coulter. Despite the fact that Adams had never before served on a corporate board and had no restaurant experience, Adams actually won. What does he plan to do with his newfound authority and power? He says he will be a watchdog for other Lone Star investors.[8]

Monitoring by Large Shareholders

Is it good for firms to have a large shareholder? Anecdotally, the answer seems to be "yes" for shareholders but "maybe not" for managers. For example, for many years Kirk Kerkorian was the largest shareholder of Chrysler and because of his large vested interest in that company he battled with former Chrysler chairman Robert Eaton for years over how the firm should be run. Eaton probably feels he has to listen to Kerkorian as Kerkorian can probably influence Eaton's salary and even job security. For example, in 1996, Kerkorian was able to force Chrysler to disburse much of its cash holdings to shareholders in the form of stock repurchases or dividends. Chrysler's minority shareholders benefit from having a fellow shareholder who is active and influential but note that Kerkorian is both active and influential probably because he is a large shareholder.

Some managers of firms can also be one of its large shareholders. For example, Bill Gates owns over 10 percent of Microsoft Corp., which probably explains why he seems to have such a strong vested interest in Microsoft's growth and financial success. Microsoft's minority shareholders directly benefit from Gates's shared interest to enhance the value of Microsoft shares. Note that a key difference between Gates being a large owner and Kerkorian being a large owner is that Gates is actually both a manager and an owner of Microsoft, while Kerkorian is simply an owner. So in the case of Microsoft a person whose wealth is significantly tied to a firm is also directly responsible for running the firm. This duality minimizes conflict of interest problems between owners and managers (note also that as a top manager, Gates can also monitor his fellow managers). In the case of Chrysler and Kerkorian, the existence of a large outside shareholder seems to exacerbate the conflicts between management and owners. However, in both cases, minority shareholders seem to come out as clear beneficiaries.

In the academic literature, large shareholders (both manager-owners and just plain owners) are in fact found to be active monitors of the firm.[9] This should not be surprising as they have the incentive *and* the power to be effective monitors. Think of it this way: if two firms are identical in every way but one firm has one or two large shareholders who own 10 percent of the firm each, while the other firm has dispersed shareholders where no single shareholder owns more than 0.1 percent of the firm, then which firm might be better monitored by its shareholders? Probably the firm with the large shareholders. It is also worth pointing out that the latter hypothetical firm probably resembles many real public firms for at least two reasons. Some public firms can be so large that it would take a lot of wealth to own a significant fraction of it. Further, most investors may not wish to forgo the benefits of portfolio diversification by investing so heavily in any one particular firm. So while large shareholders are useful monitors, there may not be a lot of investors who have the capital or the desire to be a large shareholder.

There is also a possible third reason why many firms do not have large shareholders. While large shareholders are found to be effective monitors, there is not a consensus on whether or not the presence of a large share-holder leads to higher firm values. This might be somewhat surprising but it is possible that there are firms that have a particular need for large sharehold-ers and some that do not. For example, a growth-oriented firm that is in an initial stage of its life-cycle may need monitoring by a large shareholder, while a mature firm may require less shareholder monitoring. Further, it is simply difficult to isolate the relation between shareholder activism and firm performance because so many other factors are involved. So while the importance of large shareholders on corporate governance might be unques-tioned, its importance on firm value is an on-going debate among business scholars.

Large shareholders can, of course, be institutional investors. In fact, because institutional investors have access to enormous sums of money, we generally think of them as being the large stockholders of public U.S. corporations rather than individuals. However, institutional investors may be limited in their ability to monitor the firm. This might be why the relationship between large shareholders and firm value is tenuous. We discuss these issues next.

Institutional Shareholders: An Overview

Institutional shareholders have the potential to exert effective influence. One academic study finds that proposals sponsored by institutional shareholders have a much greater chance of success than ones sponsored by individuals.[10] Fortunately, institutional shareholders, especially public pension funds, have become more active in their oversight of companies. One reason for their increased activity is their increasing ownership stakes. That is, institutional investors are large shareholders. The pie charts in Figures 7.1 and 7.2 show the percentage of U.S. equities held by different shareholder types for the years 1970 and 2002.[11]

From these charts, it can be seen that institutions now own a larger percent-age of shares than they did in 1970. The most dramatic increases are with pension funds and mutual funds. In fact, according to John Bogle, retired founder of Vanguard, just 75 funds held 44 percent of the U.S. stock market at one point during 2001.[12] As such these funds do have the economic incentive to be more active, and some actually have been.

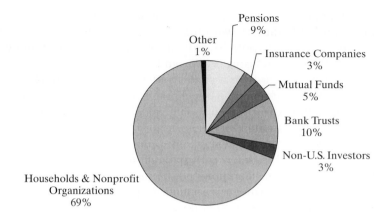

FIGURE 7.1   Shareholders of Stocks by Investor Type in 1970

Further, note that both pension funds and mutual funds actually manage money on behalf of many smaller investors. In fact, under the Employee Retirement Income Security Act (ERISA), pension funds have a fiduciary responsibility to their plan participants and beneficiaries. As such the individual investor has a right to push institutions to be more active shareholders. Pension funds in particular are in a position to be active shareholders. They have fewer restrictions compared to mutual funds, on how much of a firm they can own. Pensions can take on a relatively large ownership stake and subsequently engage in a long-term active ownership role in the firm. Therefore, not surprisingly, public pension funds often lead the way with regard to institutional shareholder activism.

FIGURE 7.2   Shareholders of Stocks by Investor Type in 2002

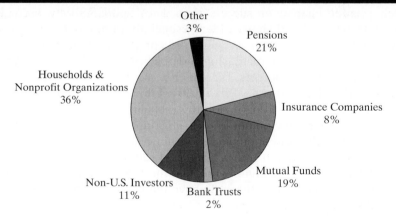

Since the early 1990s, a few public pension funds have taken on a relational investor role with a long-run mindset. These funds have tried to influence the firms they own, mainly through direct communication with management and other shareholders, by identifying poor corporate performers and through pushing for reforms.[13] For example, the public pension fund California Public Employees' Retirement System (CalPERS), which has $190 billion in assets and serves 1.4 million members, has targeted Sears and Westinghouse in the past and has pushed for them to divest laggard divisions. Also, during July 2002, the chairmen of 1,754 major U.S. firms all received a letter from the Teachers Insurance and Annuity Association College Retirement Equities Fund (TIAA-CREF), the country's largest pension fund, asking them to account for stock options as an expense.[14] Activism by TIAA-CREF is quite common; they constantly monitor firms and make numerous recommendations for reform.

To help increase their influence, many pension funds belong to a coalition called the Council of Institutional Investors (CII), whose primary objective is to help members take an active role in protecting their assets. Given that pension funds control more than $3 trillion worth of assets, they certainly do have an incentive to come together and exert influence.

DOES INSTITUTIONAL SHAREHOLDER ACTIVISM WORK?

As mentioned earlier, determining whether activism bears positive results is difficult because, more often than not, good subsequent firm performance cannot be directly linked to increased activism. According to one study commissioned by CalPERS, Steven Nesbitt of Wilshire Associates conducted a before and after analysis of 42 firms targeted for reform by CalPERS. After being targeted, the aggregate stock returns of these 42 firms over a five-year period were 52.5 percent higher than the returns of the S&P 500 Index. Prior to being targeted, these same firms had under-performed the S&P 500 by 66 percent over a five-year period.[15] Michael P. Smith of the Economic Analysis Corporation conducted an independent study of CalPERS' activism and found that the combined gain to CalPERS for their activities related to 34 targeted firms was $19 million during the 1987 to 1993 period, while the total cost to their monitoring was only $3.5 million.[16] His evidence also suggests that CalPERS' activism works.

However, counter evidence also exists. In one academic study, the authors found that shareholder proposal submission did not lead to any obvious improvements in firm performance, even for those firms where the proposals passed.[17] In a study that examined the effects of targeting by CII, the authors found no subsequent improvement for the targeted firms and little evidence of the efficacy of shareholder activism.[18] Due to the inconsistent evidence, whether activism really changes firms for the better is unknown. Perhaps one of the main problems is that activism has its own set of shortcomings, which we discuss next.

POTENTIAL ROADBLOCKS TO EFFECTIVE SHAREHOLDER ACTIVISM

Mutual funds and pension funds try to earn a high return on their portfolios. However, many active investors have a speculative or short-run view of the stock markets and they make trading and investment decisions based on short-term trends. The short-term view of these investors limits their desire to be activists.

Institutional investors might be interested in good performance for the short term and then subsequently sell the stock to move on to something else. John Bogle makes the same contention; he has been calling on mutual fund managers to engage in more activism but instead he witnesses mutual funds engaging in speculative investing. Bogle claims that during 2001, 4 out of every 10 equity funds turned their portfolio over at an annual rate of more than 100 percent.[19] If the equity funds do not like the future prospects of a firm, they simply sell the stock instead of working to change the firm.

Other than the activism of public pension funds, what about private (or corporate) pension funds? Are these groups active? Private pension funds are extremely quiet on the activism front. Jamie Heard, CEO of Institutional Shareholder Services, is not aware of a single corporate pension fund that has become a governance activist.[20] In total, private pension funds own almost 50 percent more assets than public pension funds. As a group they could be a strong monitoring force and exert influence to protect shareholders. However, private fund advisors face a huge conflict of interest problem: Corporate executives hire them to manage pension assets. If these advisors take an aggressive approach with the firm's management, then they will not be retained to manage the assets for very long. Executives probably do not want to see activism by shareholders because it interferes with their activities. Therefore they would not hire pension fund advisors who are activists. This being the case, private funds usually just go along with the firm's management, even though their fiduciary duty is supposed to be with their beneficiaries, the employees and retirees. A recent study confirms this. The authors find that mutual funds that manage a firm's 401(k) plans often voted with management.[21] In other words, mutual funds will not bite the hand that feeds them.

The regulatory and political environment may also hinder large institutional shareholders from engaging in activism. Under the Investment Company Act, mutual funds that own more than 10 percent of any one company must face additional regulatory and tax burdens. Half of the mutual fund assets must be vested in at least 20 firms (that is, a firm cannot constitute more than 5 percent of half the fund's portfolio). These ownership restrictions apply to pension funds as well. Specifically, ERISA imposes a rather strict diversification standard. As stated by Bernard S. Black, a Columbia law professor and well-known advocate of shareholder activism, ". . . pension funds are encouraged by law to take diversification to ridiculous extremes."[22]

Why do these restrictions exist? In general, the public fears having single entities with so much power. This means that funds are limited in their ability to become a major shareholder of any one firm and thus they are constrained in their ability to become stronger and more influential owners.

Bernard S. Black and another law professor, Mark J. Roe, have adamantly argued that legal restrictions stand in the way of large investors engaging in the beneficial oversight of corporations.[23] The pair contends that the legal and regulatory environment prohibits or discourages institutional investors from becoming too large, from acting together, and from becoming significant owners. At the same time these investors face tremendous SEC paperwork if they do wish to accumulate a significant stake in a firm, while also facing unfavorable tax ramifications in the process. Meanwhile, only a few laws actually encourage or make it easier for institutions to be effective owners.

INTERNATIONAL PERSPECTIVE

The public firms in the U.S. and in the U.K. have the most dispersed ownership structures in the world. This should not be surprising. For an individual investor, it costs a lot of money to own even one percent of these large, publicly traded firms. Institutional investors might have enough capital to be significant owners but they have regulatory restrictions preventing them from owning a significant fraction of any one firm.

In many other countries, however, there is greater ownership concentration where large shareholders are more prevalent. The two most common types of large shareholder are family-owners and state-owners. These large shareholders, especially family-owners, actively participate in management. For example, the Li Ka-Shing family owns and controls some of the largest firms in Hong Kong. The Wallenberg family owns and controls some of the largest firms in Sweden (such as ABB).

To own and to control the firm might seem like an optimal governance arrangement, as owner-controllers are unlikely to behave suboptimally and consequently minority (i.e. small) shareholders reap the benefits as well. However, because these owners have to be active in management and give up having diversified portfolios, there is a cost of this ownership structure to the large owners. Further, there is a chance that these family-owners may enjoy some private benefits of control (e.g. perks, large salaries, etc.) at the expense of their other smaller shareholders. That is, someone might have to monitor the family-owners.

In recent years, shareholder activist groups have begun to pop up in countries where family-ownership is prevalent. For example, the specific focus of the People's Solidarity of Participatory Democracy (PSPD), a leading shareholder activist organization that began its activism activities in the late 1990s in Korea, is to target family-owned firms (known as *chaebols*) for reform. Whether or not these shareholder activist groups will be successful remains to be seen.

Finally, it should be mentioned that a poor corporate governance infrastructure might have led to the prevalence of family-ownership and control to begin with. Some countries might not offer shareholders strong shareholder rights. With a poor governance environment, investors may have felt that they had to look out for themselves so they concentrated their wealth and maintained control. Therefore, significant governance reforms, ones that would protect minority shareholder rights, may probably have to be put in place before family-owners are willing to delegate control and diversify their wealth.

Summary

Shareholders rely on other monitors, such as the SEC, to protect their investments but they should also be more vigilant themselves. After all, it is their money and life savings. When shareholders are active monitors of the firms in which they own stocks, their activism is commonly referred to as "shareholder activism." However, it is difficult and rare for individual investors, like you, to be active and effectual. Institutional investors, on the other hand, are large shareholders, so they may be able to monitor effectively. In fact, institutional investors, such as pension funds, actually invest on behalf of their plan participants. Therefore, it could be argued that these investors should be active shareholders.

There are some institutional investors that do earnestly try to engage in shareholder activism. However, for the most part, most institutions are not active shareholders. This situation may exist because institutional investors face incentive problems, conflict of interest dilemmas, and regulatory constraints. Should we give institutional shareholders more power? Or is there a downside to them having too much ownership and power over U.S. public firms?

WEB Info about Shareholder Activism

CalPERS Shareholder Forum
www.calpers-governance.org/forumhome.asp
Council of Institutional Investors (CII)
www.cii.org
Teachers Insurance and Annuity Association College Retirement Equities Fund (TIAA-CREF)
www.tiaa-cref.org/governance/index.html

Review Questions

1. Compare and contrast the ability of different types of investors to engage in shareholder activism.
2. What can investors do to monitor and influence a company?
3. How successful is investor activism?
4. Describe the roadblocks to effective shareholder activism.

Discussion Questions

1. The text states that perhaps there are some firms that require large shareholders and some that do not. What kinds of firms might belong in each category? Might this contention apply to other monitors? How?

2. Do you think institutional shareholders should be allowed to be larger shareholders of individual firms? Why or why not?

3. Do you think there is a fair way to get more managers to own stock in their firms? Can you think of any incentive system that could be put in place to get wealthy individual investors to become large shareholders of firms?

4. In your opinion, do you think shareholder activism works? Why or why not?

Exercises

1. Do some research and describe what is involved in submitting a shareholder proposal.

2. Describe the corporate governance objectives of institutional investor activist CalPERS (or TIAA-CREF).

3. Go to the Council of Institutional Investors Web page (*www.cii.org*). What shareholder initiatives are they following?

4. Pick two firms in the same industry and identify their largest shareholders. If their ownership structure is similar or different, try to identify why this might be. Pick two firms in different industries and identify their largest shareholders. If their ownership structure is similar or different, try to identify why this might be.

5. Do some research and try to work out why the U.S. has traditionally restricted the power of institutional investors.

6. Do some research and identify and describe the current regulations that mutual funds and pension funds must adhear to. In particular, discuss regulations that might hinder their ability to be more active shareholders.

Exercises for Non-U.S. Students

1. Who are the largest shareholders in your country? How do they control the firms that they own? Do you think having these large shareholder types (e.g. the family or state) is good or bad for minority shareholders? Explain.

2. Do small individual investors have any significant power in your country? Why or why not? If not, then do you foresee improvements in this regard in the near future? Why or why not?

3. Are pension funds and mutual funds significant shareholders in your country? Why or why not?

Endnotes

1. See, for example, "Ending the Wall Street Walk," a commentary on the Corporate Governance Web site *www.corpgov.net*, or Steven Lewis, "Power to the People," *www.stevenlewis.net*.

2. Stu Gillan and Laura Starks, "Corporate Governance Proposals and Shareholder Activism: The Role of Institutional Investors," *Journal of Financial Economics* 57 (2000): 275–305.

3. Lee Clifford, "Bring Me the Head of Your Board Chairman!" *Fortune* (October 2, 2000): 252.

4. Richard Jerome, "Evelyn Y. Davis for America's Most Dreaded Corporate Gadfly," *People* (May 20, 1996).

5. David Shook, "Rebel Stockholders are on the Move," *BusinessWeek* (September 6, 2001).

6. Robert A.G. Monks and Nell Minow, "Sears Case Study," *www.lenslibrary.com*.

7. David Shook, "Rebel Stockholders are on the Move," *BusinessWeek* (September 6, 2001).

8. David Grainger, "Driving a Stake into Lone Star" *Fortune* (August 13, 2001): 32–34.

9. Perhaps the most well-known academic studies that discuss the benefits of having large shareholders include Harold Demsetz and Kenneth Lehn, "The Structure of Corporate Ownership: Causes and Consequences," *Journal of Political Economy* 93 (1985): 1155–1177; Andrei Shleifer and Robert Vishny, "Large Shareholders and Corporate Control," *Journal of Political Economy* 94 (1986): 461–488; and Randall Morck, Andrei Shleifer, and Robert Vishny, "Management Ownership and Market Valuation: An Empirical Analysis," *Journal of Financial Economics* 20 (1988): 293–315.

10. Stu Gillan and Laura Starks, "Corporate Governance Proposals and Shareholder Activism: The Role of Institutional Investors," *Journal of Financial Economics* 57 (2000): 275–305.

11. Source: NYSE Fact Book Online, *http://www.nysedata.com/factbook/main.asp*.

12. Marc Gunther, "Investors of the World, Unite!" *Fortune* (June 24, 2002): 78–86.

13. "Ending the Wall Street Walk," Corporate Governance Web site, *www.corpgov.net*: Stu Gillan and Laura Starks, "A Survey of Shareholder Activism," *Contemporary Finance Digest* 2 (1998): 10–34.

14. The letter is available for viewing on the TIAA-CREF Web site, *www.tiaa-cref.org*.

15. Source: "Ending the Wall Street Walk," Corporate Governance Web site, *www.corpgov.net*.

16. Michael P. Smith, "Shareholder Activism by Institutional Investors: Evidence from CalPERS," *Journal of Finance* 51 (1996): 227–252.

17. Jonathan M. Karpoff, Paul H. Malatesta, and Ralph A. Walkling, "Corporate Governance and Shareholder Initiatives: Empirical Evidence," *Journal of Financial Economics* 42 (1996): 365–395.

18. Wei-Ling Song, Samuel H. Szewczyk, and Assem Safieddine, "Does Coordinated Institutional Investor Activism Reverse the Fortunes of Underperforming Firms?" *Journal of Financial and Quantitative Analysis* 38 (2003): 317–336.

19. Remarks by John C. Bogle before the New York Society of Security Analysts on February 14, 2002. For the text of the speech, go to *www.vanguard.com*.

20. "Ending the Wall Street Walk," Corporate Governance Web site, *www.corpgov.net*: Stu Gillan and Laura Starks, "A Survey of Shareholder Activism," *Contemporary Finance Digest* 2 (1998): 10–34.

21. Gerald Davis and E. Han Kim, "How Do Business Ties Influence

Proxy Voting by Mutual Funds?,"
forthcoming in the *Journal of Financial
Economics.*

22. Bernard S. Black, "Institutional
Investors and Corporate Governance:
The Case for Institutional Voice," in
The Revolution in Corporate Finance,

3rd Edition (Blackwell Publishers
Oxford, UK, 1998).

23. Mark J. Roe, "Political and
Legal Restraints on Ownership and
Control of Public Companies,"
Journal of Financial Economics 27
(1990): 7–41.

CHAPTER

8

CORPORATE TAKEOVERS: A GOVERNANCE MECHANISM?

Mergers and acquisitions (M&A) are significant and dramatic events. Yet they are relatively commonplace in corporate America when compared to the rest of the world. In recent years, the U.S. has experienced some of the largest M&As ever. For example, America Online acquired Time Warner in 2001, Pfizer bought Warner-Lambert in the 2000, Exxon and Mobil merged in 1999, and SBC Communications merged with Ameritech, also in 1999. These mergers among others created some of the largest firms within their industries. During the 1990s and 2000s, the U.K. seems to be riding its own merger wave. Some of these recent large mergers have been cross-border mergers, such as Vodafone's (U.K.) acquisition of AirTouch (U.S.). Less than one year later, Vodafone Air Touch acquired Mannesmann (Germany).

The number and value of U.S. M&A transactions, for each year from 1980 to 2004, is presented in Figure 8.1. The number of acquisitions spiked in the mid-1980s; the wide availability of junk debt to finance corporate acquisitions is a common explanation for the spike. The figure also highlights the dramatic rise in M&A activity that took place during the 1990s, with a decrease in activity around the recessionary early-2000s. The figure also indicates that M&A activity has picked up since then.

There are many characteristics associated with M&As. Mergers can be characterized by:

- the type;
- the valuation of the firms involved;
- the payment;
- the new corporate structure; and
- the legal issues.

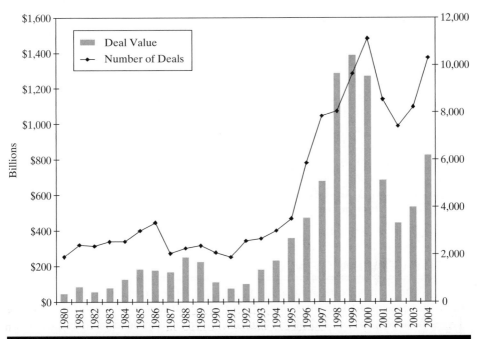

FIGURE 8.1   U.S. and U.S. Cross-Border M&A Activity Transactions

Data Source: Mergerstat

The merger type could be between firms in the same industry or different industries, or they could even be vertical mergers where a firm might acquire one of its suppliers. Participants negotiate over what is a "fair" price when a firm is trying to acquire another firm. Payment can be made with their cash holdings, borrowed money (often known as leveraged buyouts (LBOs)), and most often with newly created stocks. What will the new corporate structure look like? Who will be in charge and, which managers or business lines will be retained? Government agencies try to determine if a merger significantly reduces competition, in which case it may be deemed illegal, and therefore challenged, by the federal government. There is also the general issue of costs and benefits of conducting M&As, to both the firms and to society. Many business schools have separate courses that treat M&As as a stand-alone topic.

At this point a question that business students might ask is, "Why is a book on corporate governance discussing M&As?" During the 1980s, there were occasions where "bad" firms were acquired by other corporations and even (famously) by individual investors, who then subsequently imposed dramatic changes (such as firing the target firm's top managers) to improve the acquired firm's profitability. These kinds of corporate acquisitions were often resisted by the target firm's management because they were afraid of losing their jobs after their firms were acquired. These kinds of takeovers are often referred to as "hostile takeovers." Such hostile takeovers are sometimes known as "disciplinary takeovers" because they represent one process in which "bad" managers and/or "bad" operating procedures can be eliminated once their firms are taken over.

This chapter first provides a brief overview of M&As. However, this chapter is not about M&As *per se* so students are highly encouraged to read other corporate finance books if they wish to learn more about this exciting topic. After the brief introduction, we then discuss hostile takeovers in more detail and also characterize the nature of the disciplinary takeover. Perhaps most importantly, we then discuss how firms and their managers are able to defend against unwanted takeovers. We believe that these takeover defenses (both at the firm-level and at the U.S. state-level) may have severely hindered the disciplinary takeover market during the last two decades. We then offer some international perspective on takeovers.

BRIEF OVERVIEW OF M&A

Mergers and acquisitions can occur for a variety of reasons. Firms can merge for strategic reasons to improve operational or financial synergies. In 1999, the merger between Exxon and Mobil led to reduced oil exploration costs. Firms can merge to diversify by expanding into new businesses. The AOL and Time Warner merger brought together new and old media (i.e. AOL's internet service and Time Warner's cable (CNN, HBO) and print media (*Time, People, Sports Illustrated*)).

Mergers can be both synergistic and diversifying. The Morgan Stanley and Dean Witter merger brings together an investment bank that underwrites securities and a retail brokerage firm that sells securities. A diversifying merger can also be extreme in the sense that two very different businesses are joined together. General Electric's acquisition of the television company, NBC, during the 1980s, is a classic example of an extreme diversifying merger. Corporate diversification can make the combined firm's profits more stable but there is some debate about whether or not diversifying mergers are good for shareholders.[1]

Most of the recent mergers have occurred for growth and for increased market power. Mergers between Oracle and PeopleSoft, between Hewlett-Packard (HP) and Compaq, and between NationsBank and BankAmerica, can be viewed as market-power enhancing mergers. In recent years, these kinds of mergers seem to be popular with banks, pharmaceuticals, oil companies, and telecommunication firms. In a broad sense, we could classify all of these merger types into one category: they are *synergistic* in nature through the cutting of costs and risks and through economies of scale.

While we generally view mergers and acquisitions as being somewhat different (a merger is often viewed as a combination of two firms, whereas an acquisition is viewed as one firm buying another), almost all mergers are essentially acquisitions, as there is often an explicit buyer and seller when two firms are joined together. ExxonMobil is often thought of as a merger between equals but in reality Exxon acquired Mobil. Or put another way, Exxon "took over" Mobil. AOL purchased Time Warner. Daimler purchased Chrysler.[2]

Are corporate takeovers good for shareholders? In the first chapter, we mentioned that Hewlett-Packard's takeover of Compaq was not viewed positively by some HP shareholders nor was it viewed positively by the stock market. When HP announced its plans to acquire Compaq, HP share price immediately declined. There is a popular view that smaller firms are more nimble and more *focused* than larger firms in their ability to generate profits. In addition, some believe that managers want to take over companies simply to increase their "empire." This kind of acquisition is often referred to as "empire building." If both of these beliefs are true (and they are both widely popular beliefs), then takeovers may not be good for the acquiring firms' shareholders. Today there are people who believe that the HP-Compaq merger was bad for both of these reasons—which may be why CEO Carly Fiorina lost her job.

THE TARGET FIRM

Most of the time the "target" firm (i.e. the firm being acquired or taken over) will enjoy a share price *increase* when its acquisition is announced to the public. Why might this be? A firm, or even an individual investor, may be interested in taking over a target firm because they believe that that firm is not performing up to its full potential or that it could become an even better performer under someone else's control. The acquirer's goal under these circumstances would be to take over the firm and then to turn it around (i.e. to make it profitable) by cutting its fixed or variable costs (either by getting rid of unnecessary expenses or through financial synergy with the acquiring firm), improving its operational efficiency, or by getting rid of its "bad" managers.

Sometimes students new to finance might think it is odd that a successful firm would want to acquire an unsuccessful firm but the rationale is pretty simple. If a firm or an individual were to acquire a successful firm then they would have to pay a large sum for it and the subsequent net gains after the takeover may be limited. However, if a firm or an individual were to acquire an unsuccessful firm then they would only have to pay a relatively small sum for it. The subsequent net gains may be significant if they are able to convert the unsuccessful firm into a successful one. Unfortunately for the acquirer, because the stock market anticipates these subsequent improvements in target firms once they are taken over, the target firms' share price will *immediately* increase when its acquisition is announced. Acquirers almost always end up paying a significant premium for target firms. For example, in April 2005, Petters Group paid $12.08 a share to acquire Polaroid, whose stock was trading at $10.70 per share. An interesting debate among academics and among financial experts in general, is whether or not the premium paid for target firms is ever fully recovered. That is, does the acquisition end up being a positive NPV project for the acquirer?

Because the acquirer often pays a premium for the target firm, the target firms' shareholders might like it when their firms are taken over. However, the target firms' management team may oppose being acquired. Once firms are acquired, many of the target firm's managers are then subsequently fired so that the acquirer can install their own management team into the newly acquired firm. As you can easily imagine, corporate CEOs and presidents generally do not like being fired. When management balks at a takeover bid from an interested acquirer, the

EXAMPLE 8.1

SHAMROCK HOLDINGS FAILS IN HOSTILE TAKEOVER ATTEMPT OF POLAROID, BUT WHO IS THE REAL LOSER?

In 1988, Shamrock Holdings, an institutional investor, purchased 5 percent of Polaroid. Polaroid's stock price was trading around $30–$35 at the time. Shamrock's management team then requested a meeting with Polaroid CEO I. MacAllister Booth to discuss a friendly acquisition, but Booth stalled. Later Booth promised to meet with Shamrock management on July 13. One day before the meeting, the Polaroid board held a special meeting to approve an Employee Stock Ownership Plan (ESOP) that would account for 14 percent of Polaroid's shares. This would make it especially difficult to acquire Polaroid, as ESOP trustees are usually beholden to management. Shamrock threatened to take Polaroid to the Delaware state court, where Polaroid is incorporated, to invalidate the ESOP. In September, before the Shamrock's suit reached the courts, Shamrock made a $42 per share bid for all Polaroid shares pending a favorable outcome in court. They subsequently raised their bid to $45 per share. Polaroid management advised their shareholders to reject Shamrock's offer. In January 1989, however, the courts upheld Polaroid's ESOP. Shamrock filed an appeal. Eventually, an agreement was reached between the two firms, with Shamrock promising to drop their takeover pursuit. With all of the various concessions that Shamrock received from Polaroid in exchange for it giving up its takeover, Shamrock was able to make about $35 million in profit before taxes. Years later, in 2001, Polaroid filed for bankruptcy protection. Then, in the spring of 2005, Polaroid was bought by the Petters Group for $12.08 a share. The Polaroid CEO received $8.5 million and the Chairman received $12.8 million, while Polaroid retirees got about $47 apiece to compensate for the pension that got wiped out during Polaroid's 2001 bankruptcy.[3]

acquirer may then try to take their takeover bid directly to the target firm's large shareholders. If they can buy enough shares then they can effectively take control of the target firm and thus the target firm's management. When an interested acquirer circumvents the target firm's management, it is known as a hostile takeover. However, it can be argued that whether or not a takeover is "hostile" is in the eye of the beholder. For example, many initial hostile acquisitions are eventually approved by the target firm. Also some firms, fearing a hostile takeover, may try to work out a "friendly" deal with a potential acquirer. In both of these cases, the firms involved may publicly state that their merger was a friendly one.

The Notion of the Disciplinary Takeover

Most of the time, when a firm takes over another firm, we generally do not think of them as a "disciplinary takeover." Profitable firms can also be taken over. Time Warner was making about $27 billion in revenue when it was taken over by AOL, which was making less than $5 billion in revenue (though the merged firm is now under investigation for accounting mis-statements during the period around the merger[4]). Even hostile takeovers are not always viewed as disciplinary takeovers. PeopleSoft was a profitable firm when it was in the process of trying to take over J.D. Edwards (combined, they were expected to make about $3 billion in annual revenue) when Oracle made a hostile takeover bid for PeopleSoft during the summer of 2003.

However, because some (if not most) firms that get taken over are poorly performing firms, there are many people (such as academics) who view takeovers as an important governance mechanism. If a manager is not doing a good job, either because he is bad at managing or because he is abusing his managerial discretion (i.e. he is using his power for self-serving ends), then his firm might get taken over and he is subsequently fired. In this sense, the fear of a potential takeover might represent a powerful disciplinary mechanism to make sure that managers perform to the best of their abilities and to make sure that managerial discretion is controlled.[5] In a study of over 250 takeovers during 1958–1984, the study's authors found that over half of the target firm's top manager (usually the CEO but sometimes the president) was fired within two years of the takeover. These statistics are probably representative of today's takeover landscape. Even though Oracle's takeover of PeopleSoft might not have started off as a disciplinary takeover, many of PeopleSoft's top management team eventually got fired after Oracle's takeover. PeopleSoft's CEO, Craig Conway, was even fired just before the takeover was consummated because PeopleSoft's board felt that Conway was responsible for losing $2 billion in shareholder value.[6] While Conway's ability as a CEO can be debated, a takeover (or the fear of a takeover) represents a potentially powerful way to dismiss managers (or to motivate managers) that might not be looking out for their shareholders' best interest otherwise.

Therefore, in addition to the synergy motive for mergers mentioned previously, we could classify a second broad merger category as the disciplinary takeover. It is important to note that mergers can be for both reasons. It could easily be argued that Daimler's acquisition of Chrysler was both a synergistic merger (the two auto makers produce different types of cars and primarily serve different geographic markets) and a disciplinary takeover (Chrysler was struggling to maintain sales growth and Daimler felt that Chrysler could make a turnaround if it had Daimler-style management).

However, while takeovers may be viewed as a governance mechanism, it is not clear that they are an *effective* one. That is, we might NOT be able to rely on them as being an efficient contributor to the corporate governance system. First, as mentioned above, an acquirer may have to pay too much for a target. Second, takeovers could occur for the wrong reasons (e.g. empire building, corporate diversification). Third, even if the acquirer is able to pay a "fair" price for a target, the amount usually is still significant.

While the idea of disciplinary takeovers as a governance device might be new to some, it may be a more familiar idea to those of us who remember the "corporate raiders" of the 1980s. Corporate raiders, such as Carl Icahn and T. Boone Pickens were well known to identify firms that could not control their spending. For example, Carl Icahn took over TWA in 1985 and then dramatically cut TWA's costs. Corporate raiders are obviously *not* seeking a synergistic-type takeover; their takeovers are clearly of the disciplinary type. These disciplinary takeovers benefited target firms' shareholders. They got rid of "bad" managers and in the process they themselves also enjoyed a profit. *However*, we would be remiss if we did not mention an alternative viewpoint. These corporate raiders were also seen as villains. Because raiders often cut jobs to control costs, many people viewed raiders as heartless cost-cutters who only cared about making profits.

Once raiders obtain enough shares of a firm, they can impose their will on to them. Kirk Kerkorian, a large shareholder of DaimlerChrysler has always been an active shareholder. For example, in 1996, he forced Chrysler to disburse their large cash holdings to repurchase stock. Kerkorian's large purchase of General Motors (GM) stock, in the spring of 2005, has many analysts predicting future improvements at GM. We discussed shareholder activism in more detail in Chapter 7.

If a disciplinary takeover is profitable, in and of itself (even in the absence of a synergy motive) and if it is an effective governance mechanism, then the question that begs asking is why did we not see more of them during the 1990s and 2000s, as we did in the 1980s? Even when bad firms were taken over in recent years, a synergy-oriented reason rather than a pure investment-oriented reason, was usually cited. There are several possible reasons. First, share prices might have been inflated due to poor governance (e.g. the internet bubble, see Chapter 5), thus making disciplinary takeovers an unprofitable venture. Second, disciplinary takeovers get rid of managers whose questionable actions lead to low, not high, stock prices. For example, if a wealthy individual investor suspects that a manager is "cooking the books," then this individual may be reluctant to take over the firm whose stock price may be artificially inflated as a result of the manager's questionable acts.

Third, and mentioned previously, it costs a lot of money to buy a firm. In the 1980s, junk debt was a popular financing vehicle for takeovers but this form of capital is no longer widely available. A fourth reason, and perhaps the most important, is that today there are too many defenses against takeovers. That is, firms can install takeover defenses which may have effectively disabled this governance device from playing an active role in our corporate governance system. These takeover defenses are discussed next.

TAKEOVER DEFENSES

For the U.S., we can place takeover defenses into two categories: those at the firm-level and those at the U.S. state-level. Firm-level defenses can be broken down further into pre-emptive defenses and reactionary defenses. State-level defenses are state laws that regulate and limit takeovers. Firms lobby the state to enact such laws. We discuss firm-level takeover defenses first.

Firm-level Pre-emptive Takeover Defenses

The term **poison pill** represents any strategy that makes a target firm less attractive immediately after it is taken over. Most poison pills are simply favorable rights given to its shareholders. For example, a popularly used poison pill gives target firm shareholders the right to buy the acquirer's stock for a deep discount if its firm is acquired. Of course these rights make those firms much less attractive to takeover from the acquirer's standpoint. Other types of poison pills could involve a firm's debt becoming immediately due once it is taken over or an immediate deep-discount selling of fixed assets once it is taken over. Well over half of the S&P500 firms have a poison pill.[7]

A **golden parachute** is an automatic payment made to managers if their firm gets taken over. Because the acquirer ultimately bears the costs of these parachutes, their existence make those firms less attractive to take over. Golden parachutes can also be viewed as one type of poison pill.

A firm could have **supermajority rules** where two-thirds, or even 90 percent, of the shareholders have to approve a hand-over in control. Firms can also have **staggered boards**, where only a fraction of the board can get elected each year to multiple-year terms, thereby making it difficult to gain control of the board in any one particular year.

Firm-level Reactionary Takeover Defenses

Greenmail is a like a bribe that prevents someone from pursuing a takeover. For example, David Murdoch owned 5 percent of Occidental Petroleum in 1984 and because Occidental's management feared a hostile takeover bid by Murdoch, they bought his shares at a significant premium.[8]

Other reactionary defenses to unwanted takeover bids include the firm's management trying to convince its shareholders that the offer price is too low (from Example 8.1, note that Polaroid management did this in their defense against Shamrock's hostile takeover), raise antitrust issues, find another acquirer (also known as a *white knight*) who might not fire management after the takeover, or find an investor to buy enough shares (also known as a *white squire*) so that he can have sufficient power to block the acquisition.

State-level Anti-takeover Laws

In general there are five common state-level anti-takeover laws. **Freeze-out** laws stipulate a length of time (usually about three years) that a bidder that gains control has to wait to merge the target with its own assets. **Fair price** laws make sure that shareholders who sell their shares during a later stage of an acquisition get the same price as any other shareholder that sold their shares to the acquirer earlier. Individual firms can also adopt this type of provision. **Poison pill endorsement laws** protect the firm's rights to adopt poison pills. A **control share acquisition** law requires shareholder approval before a bidder can vote his shares. A **constituency** statute allows managers to include non-shareholders' (such as employees or creditors) interests in defending against takeovers.

Three states have rather extreme anti-takeover statutes. Pennsylvania and Ohio allow target firms to claim the short-term profits made by acquirers and Massachusetts mandates staggered boards.

There are also federal acts (e.g. Sherman Act, Clayton Act, Celler Act) that prevent mergers that would significantly reduce competition but these acts are designed to ensure a competitive environment rather than to protect firms from unwanted takeovers. This task falls to the Bureau of Competition of the Federal Trade Commission (FTC) and the Antitrust Division of the Department of Justice (DOJ). These two government agencies uphold antitrust policy. Their main focus is on anti-competitive business practices and on ensuring a competitive industry environment in the face of mergers between companies.

EXAMPLE 8.2

STATES THAT HAVE AT LEAST FOUR OF THE MENTIONED ANTI-TAKEOVER LAWS[9]:

Arizona	Florida	Georgia	Idaho
Illinois	Indiana	Kentucky	Massachusetts
Maryland	Minnesota	Missouri	New Jersey
Nevada	New York	Ohio	Oregon
Pennsylvania	Rhode Island	South Dakota	Tennessee
Virginia	Wisconsin		

EXAMPLE 8.3

ORACLE'S HOSTILE TAKEOVER OF PEOPLESOFT[10]

On June 2, 2003, PeopleSoft announced that it would be acquiring rival J.D. Edwards, which would make the combined firm the second largest enterprise application software vendor behind SAP. Four days later, Oracle, also an enterprise application software vendor, made an unsolicited offer to acquire PeopleSoft for $16 per share. PeopleSoft management issued a negative response to the bid. Twelve days later, Oracle upped the bid to $19.50 per share. Over the course of the next year and a half, numerous dramatic events played out. For one, the Department of Justice (DOJ) filed a lawsuit against Oracle citing anti-trust issues, as the merger would dramatically reduce competition in the industry. In addition to challenging the DOJ suit, Oracle was lobbying its own battles against PeopleSoft. In particular it tried to put its own slate of nominated candidates up for election to PeopleSoft's board and they challenged PeopleSoft's poison pills, one of which would have flooded the market with millions of PeopleSoft shares if it were acquired and another that would have automatically refunded PeopleSoft's customers two to five times their license fees if the firm were acquired. It was also speculated that a white knight, possibly IBM, would come to PeopleSoft's rescue. Meanwhile PeopleSoft's stock price was crumbling, prompting its board to fire its CEO, Craig Conway. At the end of 2004, PeopleSoft's board approved a takeover deal with Oracle for $26.50 per share.

ASSESSMENTS OF TAKEOVER DEFENSES

Are Takeover Defenses Bad for the Governance System?

It is hard to say whether or not these takeover defenses are the only cause of the demise of the disciplinary takeover. Most of these takeover devices (both firm-level defenses and state-level anti-takeover laws) were invented and implemented during the mid-to-late 1980s, in direct response to the high level of hostile takeovers that were taking place at the time. We may surmise, therefore, that takeover defenses at least contributed to the end of disciplinary takeovers.

If takeover defenses prevent disciplinary takeovers then their existence causes us to be left with one less governance mechanism. In this sense, takeover defenses are bad for the governance system. Studies have shown that when a firm adopts an anti-takeover mechanism, their firm's stock price declines on the news.[11] However, this is not to say that we staunchly advocate eliminating anti-takeover mechanisms. The matter is simply not clear-cut.

Corporate raiders are often looking for quick profits. We generally encourage managers and investors to have a long-run focus. Further, we can certainly sympathize with those who viewed the corporate raiders of the 1980s as heartless villains.

In the least, however, we should continue to evaluate the pros and cons of anti-takeover defenses in light of the re-evaluation of corporate governance that is taking place today. Perhaps there is a middle ground that can be achieved. Some anti-takeover devices appear only to benefit managers. For example, golden parachutes directly benefit outgoing managers, but who else? Also there is a lot of evidence that the extreme anti-takeover laws in Pennsylvania, Ohio, and Massachusetts have harmed firm value and thus shareholders.[12]

On the other hand, many firms with takeover defenses do eventually agree to be acquired. When they do the acquisition price tends to be much higher than the original offer. Therefore fighting against the merger for a while may cause the bid price to increase, thereby increasing wealth to the target firm's shareholders.

INTERNATIONAL PERSPECTIVE

The U.K. seems to be experiencing its own merger wave since the early 1990s. In fact, Vodafone's (U.K.) recent takeover of Mannesmann (Germany) is the largest ever hostile takeover. The U.S. and the U.K. probably have the most anti-takeover laws, yet they also have the most M&A activity in the world. Figure 8.2 shows the fraction of M&A activity (out of all M&A activity world-wide) that was conducted in each country in 2004. The U.S. and the U.K. comprise 60 percent of all the M&As that took place.

In bank-centered financial systems, unlike the U.S.'s capital markets system, banks seem to play a significant role in which firms merge. For example, a study finds that banks are influential in German mergers.[13] Japan is also a bank-based system and, in general, it is a country that has believed in protecting its firms from hostile takeovers, especially from foreigners.[14] However, Japan has been suffering a protracted bear market since its market crash in 1990, so it is hard to argue that its opposition to hostile takeovers has been good for shareholders (but, of course, this is not to say that M&As are the cure for Japan's economy either).

After the Asian financial crisis of 1997–1998, many Asian governments relaxed the foreign ownership restrictions of their firms. This action will attract foreign capital and at the same time a larger presence of outside investors may lead to an improvement in firm-level governance. However, whether or not the presence of outside investors (or an acquirer of an entire firm) will lead to better governance remains to be seen.

Within Asian countries and in many other countries around the world, they also have their own unique set of circumstances that make M&As difficult.

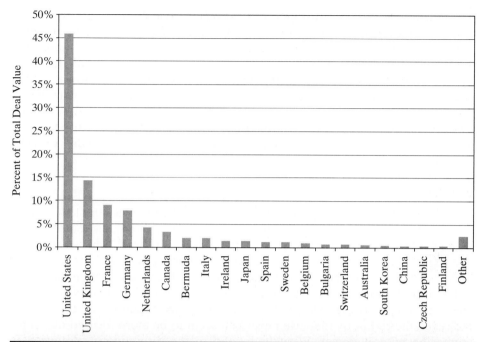

FIGURE 8.2   Percentage of Acquisition Deal Value by Country (Identified by Location of Target Firm), 2004

Data Source: ZEPHYR: published by Bureau van Dijk Electronic Publishing

EXAMPLE 8.4

THE LARGEST HOSTILE TAKEOVER DID NOT OCCUR IN THE U.S.[15]

In late October 1999, German telecommunication and engineering giant, Mannesmann, made a bid for Orange, a telecommunication firm in the U.K. Vodafone, the largest telecommunication firm in Britain, perhaps fearing a new competitor in its own backyard, responded with its own takeover bid of Mannesmann. Vodafone's Chris Gent sought out Mannesmann's Klaus Esser to make a friendly merger offer but Esser refused it. Gent then made his offer directly to Mannesmann shareholders. In the following months, a very public battle took place, where each firm took out full-page ads with each side trying to convince Mannesmann shareholders that they were in the right. In February 2000, the two firms finally agreed to merger terms and consummated the largest hostile takeover in the world.

For example, in Japan multiple corporations cross-own one another and in Korea, families are powerful controlling shareholders of many firms. Both of these arrangements make it difficult for an acquirer from outside these tight networks to take over a firm. The strength of Japan's cross-ownership has been weakening in recent years. And there is a lot of pressure on family-run businesses in Korea, from both within and outside that country, to break up their multiple business conglomerates. In the future we may see more hostile takeovers in other parts of the world but whether or not they will be viewed as an important corporate governance mechanism also remains to be seen.

Summary

In the U.S., mergers and acquisitions have been on the rise since the 1980s. In the beginning many of these acquisitions could have been characterized as hostile takeovers, as acquiring firms were looking to take over target firms whose management did not want their firm to be bought. Many of these acquirers believed they could take over a poorly performing firm and then convert them into profitable firms. In this way M&As can be viewed as a corporate governance device and thus these hostile takeovers were viewed as "disciplinary takeovers." However, the recent mergers we have seen seem to be more focused on simply increasing market power. What happened to the disciplinary takeover? In response to the hostile takeover activity of the 1980s, many firms and states adopted anti-takeover devices, thereby weakening a potentially powerful corporate governance device. Besides the U.S., takeover activity is only common in the U.K. However, given worldwide collapses in corporate governance around the world, there is a good chance that we may see a new increased worldwide M&A activity in the near future.

WEB Info about Mergers & Acquisitions

Mergerstat
www.mergerstat.com

Zephyr
www.bvdep.com/ZEPHYR.html

Bureau of Competition, Federal Trade Commission
www.ftc.gov/ftc/antitrust.htm

Antitrust Division, Department of Justice
www.usdoj.gov/atr/

Review Questions

1. What are the two broad rationales for takeovers? What are some of the specific rationales?
2. Discuss how takeovers can be viewed as a governance mechanism.
3. List and describe various takeover defenses.
4. Discuss why takeover defenses might be bad for shareholders.

Discussion Questions

1. In your opinion, who benefits when firms have takeover defenses? Who is hurt when firms have takeover defenses? In sum, which is greater, the benefits or the costs?

2. Do you believe that takeovers can effectively contribute to the corporate governance system? Why or why not?

Exercises

1. Daimler Benz was adamant that its takeover of Chrysler was really a "merger between equals." From Daimler's viewpoint, why was it important that Chrysler shareholders believed this? Do some background research.

2. Find a recent hostile takeover attempt not mentioned in this chapter. Was it successful? How did it eventually get resolved? Regardless of the outcome, do you think the target firm is now better off? Explain your answer.

3. Conduct some research and discuss the costs and benefits of state anti-takeover laws. In particular, what benefit is it to the states to have these laws?

4. Find a firm with a poison pill and describe it. Find another firm from the same industry that does not have a poison pill and try to identify why one firm has a poison pill and the other does not.

5. This chapter suggests that hostile takeovers might be good for corporate America. Do some research and try to argue that hostile takeovers are bad for corporate America.

Exercises for Non-U.S. Students

1. Compare and contrast the M&A market in your country to the U.S. Also, do some research to work out what led to the differences between the two countries (e.g. if you find that M&A activity is low in your country, then what might be the cause; is it historical, economic, social, political, ownership related, etc.?).

2. This chapter did not discuss foreign acquisitions in detail. Does your country have foreign ownership restrictions? Do you think having a more active international acquisition market can improve the corporate governance environment in your country and worldwide?

3. Do you think hostile acquisitions are going to occur more often in your country? Do you think there should be more hostile acquisitions? Support your contentions.

Endnotes

1. A firm operating in multiple and diversified businesses are known as conglomerates. A good academic article about the economic costs of diversified firms is Phil Berger and Eli Ofek, "Diversification's Effect on Firm Value," *Journal of Financial Economics* 37 (1995): 39–65. A good general article about the costs and benefits of diversified firms is Amar Bhide, "Reversing Corporate Diversification," in Donald H. Chew (ed.) *The New*

Corporate Finance, 2nd edition: Irwin McGraw Hill, (1999).

2. When two large firms join together, it is often hailed as a "merger between equals." The Daimler-Chrysler merger is an interesting case. It had been highly publicized as a merger between equals, but in fact Daimler bought Chrysler. After the merger, Daimler CEO Juergen Schrempp even stated that he too viewed the merger as a takeover. Kirk Kerkorian, the largest shareholder of Chrysler before the merger, tried to sue Daimler-Chrysler arguing that he had been misled into thinking that it was a "merger between equals" but he lost his lawsuit in 2005. More background details of the story can be found at *http://www.detnews.com/2005/ autosinsider/0504/11/C01–143977.htm*.

3. For more background details of Polaroid acquisition, see *http://www.startribune.com/stories/ 1069/5373467.html*.

4. *http://www.cfo.com/article.cfm/ 3352976/c_3353068?f= TodayInFinance_Inside*.

5. A good overview of disciplinary takeovers of the 1980s is Michael Jensen, "The Modern Industrial Revolution, Exit, and the Failure of Internal Control Systems," *Journal of Finance* 48 (1993): 831–880.

6. *http://www.eweek.com/article2/ 0,1895,1665096,00.asp*.

7. *http://207.36.165.114/Toronto/bizjak.pdf*.

8. A good description of this incident is on page 727 in Mark Grinblatt and Sheridan Titman, *Financial Markets and Strategy*, 2nd edition, Irwin McGraw Hill Publishers, 2001.

9. Grant Gartman, *State Antitakeover Laws*, Investor Responsibility Research Center, Washington DC, 2000.

10. This information comes from various news clips from *http://news.search.com/ search?q=oracle+peoplesoft& search.x=37&search.y=11*.

11. A good example of such a study is Gregg Jarrell and Annette Poulsen, "Shark Repellents and Stock Prices: The Effects of Antitakeover Amendments since 1980, *Journal of Financial Economics* 19 (1987): 127–168.

12. Sam Szewczyk and George Tsetsekos, "State Intervention in the Market for Corporate Control: The Case of Pennsylvania Senate Bill 1310," *Journal of Financial Economics* 31 (1992): 3–23, 2), Michael Ryngaert and Jeff Netter, "Shareholder Wealth Effects of the 1986 Ohio Antitakeover Law Revisited, Its Real Effects, *Journal of Law, Economics and Organization* 6 (1990): 253–262, and Robert Daines, "Do Staggered Boards Affect Firm Value? Massachusetts and the Market for Corporate Control," New York Law School working paper (2001).

13. Julian Franks and Colin Mayer, "Bank Control, Takeovers, and Corporate Governance in Germany, *Journal of Banking and Finance* 22 (1998): 1385–1403.

14. A good illustration of Japanese firms' resistance to foreign hostile takeovers is Koito Manufacturing preventing T. Boone Pickens from getting on its board. The account can be found in Kenichi Miyashita and David Russell, *Keiretsu: Inside the Hidden Japanese Conglomerates*, McGraw-Hill, 1994.

15. *http://news.search.com/search? q=vodafone+mannesmann*.

CHAPTER

9

THE SECURITIES AND EXCHANGE COMMISSION

For a while everyone enjoyed a tremendous bull market. Business seemed to be booming. Investors speculated in the stock markets, optimism was high, and some people even pondered early retirement. Then suddenly, quite dramatically, all of it changed. Large corporations went bankrupt. Corporate officers were found to be deceiving the public. Executives became engaged in courtroom battles that grabbed national headlines. As a result investors were leery of corporations and the stock markets plummeted.

While these events may sound like the late 1990s and early 2000s, they also describe the late 1920s and early 1930s. There are many examples of fraudulent behavior that can be used to illustrate those times, including unethical activities by corporate executives, securities analysts, large investors, and even newspaper reporters who hyped their own stocks. Instead of dwelling on these examples, knowing that our nation has experienced these events before is what is important.

What did the U.S. do to try to fix the investor confidence crisis during the early 1930s? The government did something quite dramatic; it decided to regulate the securities markets and created the Securities and Exchange Commission (SEC). The SEC would become the investor's advocate, putting investors on equal footing with the corporations in which they invest. When President Franklin D. Roosevelt signed the Securities Act of 1933 into law, he stated, "The Act is thus intended to correct some of the evils which have been so glaringly revealed in the private exploitation of the public's money."[1] Seventy years later, the nation finds itself again in the midst of an investor confidence crisis. In response to the crisis, the U.S. again passed a sweeping securities Act, known as the Sarbanes-Oxley Act. When President George W. Bush signed the act into law in 2002, he stated, "corporate corruption has struck at investor confidence, offending the conscience of our nation. . . And today I sign the most far-reaching reforms of American business practices since the time of Franklin Delano Roosevelt. . . The American economy depends on fairness and honesty. The vast majority of businesses uphold those values. With this law, we have new tools to enforce those values, and we will use those tools aggressively to defend our free enterprise system against corruption and crime."[2]

Corporations in the U.S. are regulated by many governmental agencies. For example, the Federal Trade Commission (FTC) regulates advertising by businesses and the Food and Drug Administration (FDA) approves pharmaceutical company drug sales, all to protect consumers. What makes the SEC different from other business overseers is its role of protecting investors. Therefore the SEC is an important component of the corporate governance system. This chapter provides an overview of the SEC by describing the securities acts, the SEC organizational structure, and the difficulties it has in effectively carrying out its monitoring role.

THE SECURITIES ACTS

There are seven major laws that govern the securities industry, which the SEC oversees. The first is the **Securities Act of 1933**. This act requires firms to register securities intended for public sale. The most common securities registration form is called **Form S-1**. In the registration form, the firm must describe the securities for sale, an estimate of and specific purposes of the sale's proceeds, and the underwriting arrangement. In addition, the firm also has to provide a general overview of itself, including a description of the nature of its business, balance sheet and operating income information, and details of its management and management compensation. No information can be fraudulent or deceitful. All statements are made publicly available. The information in the registration form helps potential investors make informed investing decisions.

The **Securities Exchange Act of 1934** created the SEC and gave it authority to oversee the securities industry, including large shareholders (defined as shareholders that own at least 5 percent of a firm), brokerage firms, securities dealers, and the stock exchanges. The 1934 Act is broader in scope than the 1933 Act. As part of the 1934 Act, brokers, dealers, and stock exchanges must register with the SEC and file periodic reports. Just as important, public corporations are also required to submit periodic reports under the Act, including annual reports known as **10-Ks** and quarterly reports known as **10-Qs**. In a way these reports are updates of the firms' securities registration forms required under the 1933 Act. Since 1996, all public firms had to file their 10-Ks and 10-Qs electronically using the Electronic Data Gathering, Analysis, and Retrieval (EDGAR) system. These company filings can be viewed by anyone on the SEC website, *www.sec.gov*.

In addition to the periodic filings, if significant changes or events take place in between the time these files are submitted, then the firm must file update forms known as **8-Ks**. Examples of significant corporate events that prompt these filings include entering or terminating material business agreements, new financial obligations, change in exchange listing status, and sales of unregistered securities. For example, if a firm agrees to settle a lawsuit against it with a cash payment then the firm must file an 8-K describing the nature of the event, the amount to be paid, and the source of the payment. The 1934 Act also allows the

SEC to govern the proxy process (this is the process used to solicit shareholder votes on director elections or to approve corporate actions) and the insider trading that takes place among the firm's executives and other inside parties.

The **Trust Indenture Act of 1939** applies to the sale and formal agreement between buyer and seller of debt securities. The **Investment Company Act of 1940** regulates investment companies such as mutual funds by requiring the disclosure of their financial condition and their investment policies. The **Investment Advisors Act of 1940** currently regulates investment advisors who manage more than $25 million or who advise a registered investment company. Finally, the **Public Utility Holding Company Act of 1935** regulates gas and electric holding companies.

In the summer of 2002, the Sarbanes-Oxley Act, otherwise known as the **Public Company Accounting Reform and Investor Protection Act of 2002**, was signed into law. This new law sets up a new oversight body to regulate auditors, creates laws pertaining to corporate responsibility, and increases punishments for corporate white-collar criminals. The main aspects of this act are as follows (a more detailed discussion of this Act is presented in Chapter 10).

1. The legislation establishes a non-profit corporation called the Public Company Accounting Oversight Board, which will operate under SEC discretion, to oversee the audit of public companies and to protect the interests of investors and the general public by improving audit report accuracy.
2. The Act attempts to protect investors by breaking the relationships among auditors, consultants, and the public company being audited.
3. The Act increases the monitoring ability and responsibilities of boards of directors and improves their credibility by making boards more independent and more responsible for audits.
4. The Act tries to make executive actions more transparent to shareholders by requiring the disclosure of "off-balance-sheet transactions" and decreasing the time to two days that an executive has to report company stock (and other equity) trades to the SEC.
5. The legislation makes it easier to prosecute executive criminal behavior in the future by spelling out new or altered definitions of criminal behaviors and it stiffens penalties.

The 2002 Act's Effect on Accounting Oversight

With the 2002 Act's establishment of the Public Company Accounting Oversight Board (PCAOB), the SEC's oversight over public accounting has dramatically expanded. As discussed in Chapter 10, the Financial Accounting Standards Board (FASB) and the American Institute of Certified Public Accontants (AICPA) were primarily responsible for governing accounting standards and overseeing audits. In 1973, the SEC appointed FASB, a non-government entity made up of members of the accounting, business, and academic professions, to set accounting standards. Its standards are known as Generally Accepted Accounting Principles (GAAP). The SEC also required that all public firms be audited by Certified Public Accountants (CPAs) who had to make sure that audited firms complied with GAAP. To oversee this process, the SEC had granted authority to the AICPA to govern external auditors (i.e. public accounting firms) and to set auditing standards. Since the enactment of the 2002 Act, however, the AICPA lost its authority to oversee public company audits to the SEC's new PCAOB.

The PCAOB is an non-proift entity whose financing comes from firms registered with the SEC and from public accounting firms. Under the 2002 Act, all public firms have to be registered with PCAOB and meet its standards. The PCAOB oversees the public accounting firms as well. The board consists of five members appointed by the SEC but while all five members must be finance literate, what is interesting is that only two can be or have been a CPA.

Summary of the Acts

Note that all of the acts taken together, especially the first two (the 1933 and 1934 Acts) and the last one (the 2002 Act), simply boil down to the following: The acts force corporations to tell the public about themselves and they cannot lie. This way investors can then make informed decisions. In addition, the spirit of the acts is to put investors' interests first. As such, the SEC represents the primary external regulatory body responsible for corporate governance, especially now given that its role in overseeing public accounting has expanded under the 2002 Act.

ORGANIZATIONAL STRUCTURE OF THE SEC

Headquartered in Washington, D.C., the SEC has 11 regional and district offices. These offices are located in Atlanta, Boston, Chicago, Denver, Fort Worth, Los Angeles, Miami, Philadelphia, Salt Lake City, San Fransisco, and New York City. The commission consists of 4 divisions and 18 offices and employs over 3,100 people.

At the top of the organizational chart are the commissioners. Five commissioners each serve a five-year term. The U.S. president appoints these people and the Senate must approve them. Appointments occur annually and there is one appointment per year because the terms are staggered. No more than three commissioners can belong to the same political party. One commissioner serves as chairman, the top SEC executive, and is also designated by the president. The current SEC Chairman is Christopher Cox who took the helm in August 2005. He replaced William H. Donaldson who took over the SEC's leadership role following Harvey Pitt's departure, whose tenure at the SEC helm lasted only 18 months (from August 2001 to February 2003) due to political pressure stemming from the massive corporate scandals.

Figure 9.1 shows the four divisions that are the pillars of the SEC. The **Division of Corporate Finance** oversees corporate disclosure, ensuring that the public has all relevant information necessary to make investment decisions. Full

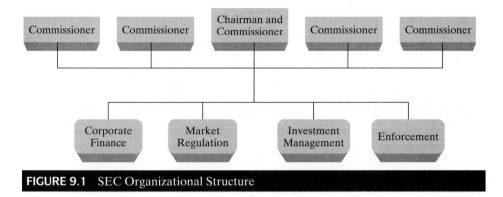

FIGURE 9.1   SEC Organizational Structure

corporate disclosure encompasses the registration statements of securities for sale, annual and quarterly reports, proxy materials, and annual reports to shareholders. Because the Division of Corporate Finance reviews the documents required under the 1933, 1934, and 2002 Acts, many people tend to think of this Division as being the SEC's primary division.

The **Division of Market Regulation** oversees securities markets participants, such as the brokerage firms and their agents, and the stock exchanges under the Investment Advisors Act of 1940. The Division of Market Regulation is specifically responsible for curtailing securities fraud, for ensuring high quality securities transactions on exchanges, and for ensuring proper conduct by securities dealers.

The **Division of Investment Management** assists the SEC with the Investment Company Act of 1940, the Investment Advisors Act of 1940, and the Public Utility Holding Act of 1935. Specifically, the Division of Investment Management is the primary regulator of investment companies. Finally, the **Division of Enforcement** investigates possible violations of securities laws. The SEC has only civil enforcement authority but it can also play a crucial role in helping federal agencies pursue criminal charges for severe violations of the law. Each year the SEC prosecutes between 400 and 500 individuals and companies for wrongdoing, with most of these prosecutions being settled out of court. These violations mainly involve accounting fraud, insider trading, and deception regarding securities. A sample litigation release from a recent settlement between HealthSouth Corporation and the SEC is shown in Example 9.1.

The 18 SEC offices mostly deal with SEC internal affairs, such as personnel, or serve as advisors (e.g. general counsel and economists) for the divisions and the SEC commissioners. The other responsibilities of these offices are varied, including the handling of compliance inspections, investor education, and international affairs. Perhaps the most notable among the offices is the **Office of the Chief Accountant**, which works closely with FASB and PCAOB, and is the primary advisory office to the SEC on matters of accounting.

EXAMPLE 9.1

HEALTHSOUTH CORPORATION AND THE SEC

U.S. SECURITIES AND EXCHANGE COMMISSION

Litigation Release No. 19280 / June 23, 2005

Accounting and Auditing Enforcement
Release No. 2263 / June 23, 2005

*SECURITIES AND EXCHANGE COMMISSION V. HEALTHSOUTH
CORPORATION ET AL.*, Civil Action No. CV-03-J-0615-S

FINAL JUDGMENT ENTERED AGAINST HEALTHSOUTH CORP., INCLUDES
ANTI-FRAUD INJUNCTION, $100 MILLION PENALTY, CREATION OF
INSPECTOR GENERAL REPORTING TO AUDIT COMMITTEE OF THE BOARD,
AND OTHER RELIEF IN CONNECTION WITH THE HEALTHSOUTH CORP.
ACCOUNTING FRAUD

On June 22, 2005, the Honorable Inge Prytz Johnson, United States District
Judge for the Northern District of Alabama, entered a final judgment against
HealthSouth Corporation, enjoining it from violating Section 17(a) of the
Securities Act of 1933 and Sections 10(b), 13(a), 13(b)(2)(A) and 13(b)(2)
(B) of the Securities Exchange Act of 1934 and Rules 10b-5, 12b-20, 13a-1,
and 13a-13 thereunder. The judgment will also require HealthSouth to (i)
pay a civil penalty of $100 million, with $12.5 million payable by October 15,
2005, and additional payments of $12.5 million by April 15, 2006, $25 million
by October 15, 2006, $25 million by April 15, 2007 and $25 million by October
15, 2007; (ii) disgorge $100; (iii) pay the costs of any distribution of
disgorgement and penalties to investors; (iv) retain a consultant to review
its corporate governance practices; (v) retain a consultant to review its
accounting controls, or as an alternative to an accounting consultant,
provide to the Commission's staff communications from HealthSouth's
auditors and others regarding its controls and report on its actions to
correct deficiencies; (vi) appoint and provide staff for an Inspector General
to report to the audit committee of HealthSouth's board of directors; (vii)
implement training programs for officers and employees involved in
accounting and financial reporting and for senior operations executives at
the corporate, division and subsidiary levels, to educate such officers and
employees and prevent future violations of the securities laws; and (viii)
continue to cooperate with the on-going government investigations. The
Commission's complaint, filed on March 19, 2003 and amended April 3, 3003,
alleged that shortly after the company became public in 1986, the company
began to artificially inflate its earnings to meet Wall Street analysts'
expectations and maintain the market price for HealthSouth's stock and that
since 1999, HealthSouth systematically overstated its earnings by at least
$1.4 billion.

HealthSouth, in consenting to the judgment, neither admitted nor denied the
allegations of the complaint. HealthSouth provided substantial cooperation in
connection with the investigation of this matter. The penalty amount will be
distributed to defrauded investors pursuant to the Fair Funds provision of
Sarbanes-Oxley.

See also: L. R. 18,044/March 20, 2003; L.R. 18059/April 1, 2003; L.R.
18060/April 1, 2003; AAER No. 1749/April 1, 2003; L.R. 18070/April 4, 2003;
L.R. 18339/September 10, 2003; L.R. No. 18700 and AAER No. 2004/May 10,
2004; L.R. 18843/August 23, 2004; L.R. No. 18904/September 28, 2004

http://www.sec.gov/litigation/litreleases/lr19280.htm

NEED FOR THE ACTS AND THE SEC

Opinions regarding the SEC vary. Businesses and the securities industry are not always happy with SEC decisions. In addition, the costs of reporting and following SEC regulations, in general, are tremendous. Byron C. Radaker, CEO of Congoleum Corporation, took his company private in the early 1980s, citing that this would save his firm between $6 and $8 million per year in reporting costs.[3] While companies may not appreciate the SEC, the question that needs to be asked is can investors do without it? In order to consider this we must first think about the thrust of the Securities Acts.

Many people, especially academics, believe that the stock markets are "efficient." What does this mean? The notion of market efficiency is that current stock prices reflect their fundamentally correct value. To understand this concept consider this point: Millions of people participate in the stock markets. The average of their beliefs and opinions, based on current and past information, will be reflected in the current stock price. For example, if a stock price is too low, some people out of the millions would recognize this and rush to buy the stock. Because of the buying, the stock price would rise and not be undervalued for long. Millions of market participants continuously process information which, in turn, makes the markets efficient. If markets are efficient then do we really need the SEC?

In the context of market efficiency, if companies do hide facts or lie, then someone will find out because many people are involved, including brokers, analysts, directors, employees, accountants, creditors, investors, and even state regulators. Thus the inevitable revelation of fraud will cause the stock price to plummet. Besides, companies that lie and get caught cannot last anyway. We have always had a climate where consumers and investors have cast a suspicious eye toward large businesses.

Some finance scholars have attempted to assess empirically the importance of SEC regulation to our financial markets. In 1964, George Stigler, who would later go on to win the Nobel Prize in economics, published a famous study in which he compared new securities being issued in the 1920s to those issued in the 1950s, to determine whether the existence of the SEC had improved the securities markets.[4] He found no difference and he contended that SEC regulation did not improve the quality of the securities markets. However, two other professors subsequently countered Stigler's study, citing that securities fraud decreased because of the existence of the SEC.[5] This debate continues today. In 1995, in response to market participants' complaints regarding regulatory costs and excessive regulatory burdens, the SEC formed a committee to study the feasibility of making it less burdensome for established public firms to issue securities.[6] In 1998, the SEC issued such a proposal but it was not enacted.

Overall we may never know for sure if the SEC does make our securities markets better. Perhaps markets would still be efficient without the SEC. However, the very existence of the SEC might contribute to market discipline and thus market efficiency. Consider, for instance, that whenever the SEC makes enforcements actions against public firms for disclosure violations or other Securities Acts violations, the stock price of those firms decline upon hearing the news. So the SEC at least has some "teeth" as a disciplinarian.[7]

SEC PROBLEM AREAS

Reporting

One issue that people question is the adequacy of quarterly and annual reporting. If the information is to be useful then there may need to be more frequent reporting. We now live in a world where technology permits us to access information, especially up-to-date information, on a continuous basis. Why not take advantage of this? Of course, frequent reporting would cause an outcry by corporate America, which already complains about reporting costs but there may be several viable ways to address this issue. One approach that is perpetually under consideration is to require companies to submit their reports earlier.[8] Instead of providing a deadline of 90 days after the close of the fiscal year for filing of annual reports, it could be 60 days. For quarterly filings the deadline could be shortened to 30 days instead of 45. However, this suggestion might not be ideal. Note that the report frequency may still be the same but the timing would improve. Also, as pointed out in a *Business Week* commentary, this proposal might only add concerns about the haste and thus the accuracy with which companies compile reports.[9] Another way to address the problem of infrequent reporting is to force companies to reveal immediately any material information that investors will deem important.[10] In fact, since March 2004, the SEC now requires 8-Ks to be filed within 4 instead of the previous 5 to 15 business days after the triggering event.

Punishment

Others believe that the SEC may be too weak because it cannot pursue criminal prosecution. Note that the SEC has the authority to bring civil charges only. If criminal prosecution can serve as a key deterrent to corporate crime then there may be some truth to the notion that the SEC does not really have the policing power necessary to do its job. However, this problem may not be critical. The SEC can easily persuade prosecutors to bring criminal charges once it has evidence that the case has merit. Also keep in mind that prosecuting corporate criminals is difficult. As pointed out in the July 1, 2002, issue of *Business Week*,[11] securities laws are ambiguous, sophisticated financial concepts that are difficult to grasp and executives have plenty of tricks up their sleeves to absolve themselves of responsibility (e.g. "I didn't know that the books were fraudulent."). Therefore, in light of current difficulties with criminal charges, giving an additional agency, such as the SEC, the additional responsibility of bringing criminal charges might not make sense.

Having civil charge authority only, the primary punishment tool employed by the SEC is to fine companies for wrongdoing. Heavier and heavier fines seem to be levied. Critics argue that when individuals, such as corporate executives, commit fraud, they should be punished. Yet it is often the company that gets fined. Ultimately those fines are paid by the shareholders because it comes out of the companies profits. Shareholders end up suffering twice—once when the stock price falls as news of the wrong doing is released and again when the company must pay the fines for the wrong-doing. Indeed, managers often deflect an SEC investigation by offering to pay a fine with the company's money.

Consider that the SEC investigated Bristol-Myers Squibb for accounting fraud in 2002. This led to a 50 percent decline in stock price (a loss of about $40 billion in market capitalization) in the ensuing months and a restatement of earnings in 2003, which included a lowering of reported sales for 1999 to 2001 by $2.5 billion. In August of 2004, after a two-year investigation, Bristol-Myers agreed to settle SEC civil charges by paying a $150 million fine.[12] After seeing their firm loose $40 billion in value because of the accounting fraud allegations, the shareholders will lose another $150 million as punishment for the executives' behavior.

SEC Resources

Another problem may be that the commission was, and maybe still is, under-funded. Being under-funded has two repercussions. First, the SEC may be hindered in its ability to hire and retain the best staff. One estimate had put the pay of SEC attorneys and examiners at as much as 40 percent less than their peers at comparable federal agencies.[13] In 2001, Congress did give approval to the SEC to pay its lawyers and accountants salaries that are competitive with other government banking agencies, such as the Federal Reserve. The increase in budget from the passage of the Public Company Accounting Reform and Investor Protection Act of 2002 ended up being much larger, more than $300 million, than the previous budget.

For a long time the SEC has had the distinction of being an important stepping-stone for many young ambitious and talented attorneys and accountants, who usually can count on the experience to command much higher salaries elsewhere. These talented people gain experience and a name for themselves at the SEC and then they are hired by the very law firms that represent companies, auditing firms, and individuals that deal with the SEC. According to one estimate, the SEC employee turnover rate is 30 percent, which is double the rate for the rest of the government. Losing talent shortens the SEC's institutional memory and the average experience of its key employees, while it increases the time and money needed to train new hires.

A second repercussion of being under-funded is being under-staffed. Since 1993, the SEC's workload has almost doubled but staffing levels have been stagnant.[14] Former SEC Commissioner Laura S. Unger once admitted that there were only about 100 lawyers that reviewed the disclosure documents of the 17,000 public firms.[15] An SEC chief accountant stated that only 1 out of 15 annual reports is reviewed. While it may be impossible for the SEC ever to be able to pursue and investigate thoroughly all possible violations, a larger staff would definitely be able to do more. In light of the recent crisis, the SEC has tripled the number of probes.[16] However, overworking the current staff cannot last forever. Fortunately, the Public Company Accounting Reform and Investor Protection Act of 2002 mandated that the SEC hire hundreds more people.

EXAMPLE 9.2

ARTHUR LEVITT'S "I TOLD YOU SO"

Arthur Levitt served as SEC chairman from 1993 to 2001 and he was often criticized by business—both corporate America and the accounting profession attacked him. This situation is probably why a September 2000 issue of *Business Week* dubbed Levitt the "Investor's Champion."[17]

Levitt was known as a tough regulator whose victories included censuring the National Association of Securities Dealers for collusive pricing practices, which resulted in NASDAQ dealers having to pony up more than $1 billion to settle the case. Another was the adoption of Regulation Fair Disclosure, which put an end to corporate officers tipping off analysts. Toward the end of his tenure, one of his main causes was to clean up the accounting profession. In a famous speech delivered at New York University on September 28, 1998, Levitt called for an end to the "numbers game."[18] Levitt felt that corporate managers, auditors, and analysts participated in the process of managing earnings, using a variety of tricks (he called them "nods and winks") to meet earnings estimates, all at the expense of high quality full disclosure. He felt that this game had to stop and accountants needed to make numbers more reliable and to have the trust of the investing public.

Levitt felt strongly that one way to clean up the accounting profession, which in the late 1990s was facing a slew of accounting scandals, would be to separate the accountant's role as auditor and consultant for the same firm. Levitt felt that this was a huge conflict of interest. Of course there was a tremendous backlash from both corporate America, which claimed that accountants who consult for them are in the best position to audit them and from the accounting industry, which did not want to see profitable consulting practices taken away. Less than two years later, on June 27, 2000, the SEC unanimously approved issuing Levitt's proposal. In the end Congress defeated the proposal. Then two years later, Congress passed most of Levitt's proposals in the Sarbanes-Oxley Act of 2002. Senator Robert Torricelli, a New Jersey democrat, told Levitt on January 24, 2002, "We were wrong. You were right."[19]

INTERNATIONAL PERSPECTIVE

Earlier it was mentioned that we could not know for certain whether or not the U.S. is better off having the SEC. However, one way we can get some insight into the importance of securities regulation would be to compare countries that have a strong securities regulator and/or regulations to those countries that do not. A couple of new academic studies do just that. In a recent study, the authors examine the quality of securities laws in 49 countries.[20] They create two broad indices. First, they assess the strength of the countries' public securities regulator (i.e. an institution such as the U.S. SEC) by measuring the regulators' autonomy (i.e. are they free from political interference), by whether or not they are primarily focused on stock markets, by their ability to issue rules, by their ability to investigate potential rule violations, and by their ability to impose sanctions on violators. Based on these criteria, the researchers create an index that they call the "public enforcement index."

Second, they assess the countries' quality of disclosure (e.g. on prospectuses of new securities issues, information on compensation, information on ownership structure, etc.) and the relative burden of proof required by investors seeking retribution from firms (in particular, for the omission of material information on prospectuses). Based on these two criteria, they create an index that they call the "private enforcement index."

Overall they find that countries' quality of public enforcement is unrelated to stock market development. In contrast, countries' quality of private enforcement is strongly related to their stock market development. Their findings suggest that securities laws do matter but probably not as much as many of us would have thought.

The authors of another study use a different criteria to measure the quality of securities laws and find that when law quality is higher the country

---

EXAMPLE 9.3

QUALITY OF REGULATOR AND SECURITIES LAWS

Countries with the best and worst public enforcement:

BEST	WORSE
Australia	Austria
Hong Kong	Belgium
Singapore	Japan
U.S.	Switzerland

Countries with the best and worst private enforcement:

BEST	WORSE
Canada	Austria
Philippines	Ecuador
Singapore	Uruguay
U.S.	Venezuela

enjoys a lower cost of equity, higher liquidity for securities, and superior market price efficiency.[21] This latter study suggests that securities laws are beneficial.

Summary

The SEC's main function is to oversee the federal securities acts, which mandate that public corporations tell the public about themselves and that they do so honestly. The SEC also reviews documents filed in accordance with the Acts and investigates potential violations of its acts. Therefore the SEC is an important corporate monitor; in fact, this work is its explicit designated function. The SEC seems to be a powerful and effective monitor but it has encountered some problems in the performance of its duties. It may be over-worked, under-funded, and under-staffed. In addition it only has civil powers to punish wrongdoers, not criminal powers. This leads to a focus of levying fines against corporations where executives have been charged with committing fraud. In the end, shareholders suffer from both the wrongdoing itself and the SEC punishment. The Sarbanes-Oxley Act of 2002 gives the SEC more money and power but will it be enough?

WEB Info about the SEC

U. S. Securities and Exchange Commission
www.sec.gov
SEC Filings & Forms (EDGAR)
www.sec.gov/edgar.shtml
SEC's Office of Investor Education and Assistance
www.sec.gov/investor.shtml

Review Questions

1. Name and describe the Acts that are overseen by the SEC that governs the securities industry.
2. Describe the organizational structure and the primary functions of the SEC.
3. What are the main problems that the SEC has encountered in trying to perform its duties?

Discussion Questions

1. The 2002 Act is discussed in more detail in Chapter 10. At this point, what is your opinion of the Act? Explain.
2. Do you think we need more or less securities regulation? If more, then do you have any good ideas for additional ones? If less, then which regulations would you eliminate and why?

Exercises

1. Do some research and try to figure out what led to the appointments of the last three SEC Chairmen. Was it political? Was it their professional backgrounds? Describe some of their noteworthy and significant influence and work while at the SEC.

2. Go to the SEC web site (*www.sec.gov*) and use the EDGAR system to download a 10-Q filing for a large U.S. firm. What does the filing reveal about the firm's operations, its management team, and its financial condition?

3. Go to the SEC web site (*www.sec.gov*). Go to the regulatory actions link and describe some of the proposed and final rule changes. Why are they being implemented?

4. Find a firm that is currently undergoing an SEC investigation (or has recently settled a suit with the SEC). Describe the issues and circumstances involved. Is, or was, any other government agency, such as the Department of Justice or New York's Attorney Gerenal's Office, involved? If so, then explain their (or its) involvement.

5. With the passage of the 2002 Act, the SEC was granted a much larger operating budget. Provide a progress report. Has the SEC reviewed more filings? Investigated more securities violations? Hired more people?

6. Provide a progress report on the new Public Company Accounting Company Oversight Board. Has it started functioning? What are its priorities?

Exercises for Non-U.S. Students

1. Describe securities regulation in your country. In your opinion, does it impose high quality regulations?

2. Does your country's securities regulator follow through with effective enforcement of its laws? Describe the last time they prosecuted any person or firm for a securities violation.

3. To what extent do you think politics contributes to the quality of securities laws in your country? Explain.

4. To what extent do you think the securities regulator has contributed to the success or failure of your country's securities markets? Explain.

Endnotes

1. Joel Seligman, *The Transformation of Wall Street*, (Boston, MA: Northeastern University Press, 1995).

2. *http://www.whitehouse.gov/news/releases/2002/07/20020730.html*.

3. Cited in Eugene F. Brigham and Michael C. Ehrhardt, *Financial Management*, 10th Edition. Harcourt Publishers, Orlando, FL, (2002): 759.

4. George J. Stigler, "Public Regulation of the Securities Markets," *Journal of Business* 37 (1964): 117–142.

5. Irwin Friend and Edward S. Herman, "The SEC Through a Glass Darkly," *Journal of Business* 37 (1964): 382–405.

6. See unpublished paper by Hyun-Han Shin, "The SEC's Review of the Registration Statement and Stock Price Movements during the Seasoned Equity Issuance Process," (Ph.D. diss., Ohio State University, 1995).

7. Mahmoud M. Nourayi, Stock Price Responses to the SEC's Enforcement

Actions, *Journal of Accounting and Public Policy* 13 (1994): 333–347.

8. Judy Mathewson, James L. Tyson, and David Evans, "Harvey Pitt: Odd Man Out on Enron," *Bloomberg Markets* (March 2002): 51–56.

9. Mike McNamee, "The SEC's Accounting Reforms Won't Answer Investor's Prayers," *Business Week* (June 17, 2002): 28.

10. Judy Mathewson, James L. Tyson, and David Evans, "Harvey Pitt: Odd Man Out on Enron," *Bloomberg Markets* (March 2002): 51–56.

11. Mike France and Dan Carney, "Why Corporate Crooks Are Tough to Nail," *Business Week* (July 1, 2002): 35–38.

12. Lewis Krauskopf, "Charged with Accounting Fraud, Bristol-Myers Squibb Settles for $150 Million," *Knight Ridder Tribune Business News* (August 5, 2004): 1.

13. Joseph Nocera, "System Failure," *Fortune* (June 24, 2002): 62–72.

14. Mike McNamee and Amy Borrus, "The Reluctant Reformer," *Business Week* (March 25, 2002): 72–81.

15. Joseph Nocera, "System Failure," *Fortune* (June 24, 2002): 62–72.

16. Mike McNamee and Amy Borrus, "The Reluctant Reformer," *Business Week* (March 25, 2002): 72–81.

17. Cover story in *Business Week* (September 25, 2000).

18. The full text of Levitt's speech is available on *www.rutgers.edu/raw/aaa/newarc.*

19. Judy Mathewson, James L. Tyson, and David Evans, "Harvey Pitt: Odd Man Out on Enron," *Bloomberg Markets* (March 2002): 51–56.

20. Rafael LaPorta, Florencio Lopez-de-Silanes, and Andrei Shleifer, "What Works in Securities Laws?" forthcoming in the *Journal of Finance* (2006).

21. Hazem Daouk, Charles Lee, and David Ng, "Capital Market Governance: How do Security Laws affect Market Performance?" forthcoming in the *Journal of Corporate Finance* (2005).

10 NEW GOVERNANCE RULES

I n July of 2002, the U.S. passed the Sarbanes-Oxley Act, otherwise known as the Public Company Accounting Reform and Investor Protection Act of 2002. Sarbanes-Oxley is without question the most dramatic federal law pertaining to corporate governance since the initial securities laws of the 1930s. In addition to the enormous scope of the law, the speed with which it went through the legislative process might also be considered equally impressive. Political economists have noted that the U.S. often responds with new legislation when stock markets and thus public opinion of businesses are down.[1] In this case the legislators probably also felt significant political pressure to respond quickly to the investor confidence crisis, as 2002 was an election year. However, acting quickly can often come at the expense of acting carefully, thoughtfully, and rationally. This chapter first provides an overview and discussion of the Sarbanes-Oxley Act. Then it provides an overview of the new NYSE and NASDAQ corporate governance rules imposed on their listed firms. A brief history documenting how market conditions lead to both the strengthening and the relaxing of securities regulations in the U.S. is presented. Finally, the chapter concludes by illustrating that the trend for increasing corporate governance standards was a global trend.

SARBANES-OXLEY ACT OF 2002

Sarbanes-Oxley, a bill drafted by Democratic Senator Paul Sarbanes and Republican Congressman Michael Oxley, was signed into law by U.S. President George W. Bush on July 30, 2002. Overall, the Act created a new oversight body to regulate auditors, created laws pertaining to corporate responsibility, and increased punishments for corporate white-collar crime. The following sections describe each aspect of the Act.

Public Company Accounting Oversight Board

The Act establishes a non-profit corporation called the Public Company Accounting Oversight Board to oversee the audit of public companies, in order to improve the accuracy of audit reports. The Board operates under the discretion of the SEC. The duties of the Board are to:

1. register public accounting firms;
2. establish or adopt auditing quality control, ethics, independence, and other standards;
3. conduct inspections of public accounting firms;
4. conduct investigations, disciplinary proceedings, and sanctions of accounting firms where justified;
5. promote high professional standards and improve the quality of audit services;
6. enforce compliance of the rules of the Board, professional standards, and securities laws in regard to auditing; and
7. oversee the budget and manage the operations of the Board.

The five members of the Board will be employed full time by the Board and will exhibit independence from the public accounting firms being regulated. Only two of the Board members can be (or have been) a CPA.

Auditor Independence
Sarbanes-Oxley also tries to ensure auditor independence. This aspect of the Act attempts to address one of the core problems with auditors being monitors of the firm (see Chapter 3). To accomplish this goal, the Act does the following:

1. prohibits accounting firms from providing both auditing and consulting activities for the same firm;
2. gives the audit committee of the company's board of directors more authority over auditing activities;
3. forces the lead audit partner in an audit team to change at least every five years;
4. disallows auditing by an accounting firm if any of the top executives of the public company were employed by the accounting firm within the past year; and
5. requires a study to be conducted that investigates the potential outcomes of mandatory rotation of accounting firms conducting audits.

Corporate Responsibility
Sarbanes-Oxley also attempts to increase the monitoring ability and responsibilities of boards of directors and improve their credibility. Specifically the Act does the following:

1. makes the audit committee of the board of directors both more independent from management and more responsible for the hiring and oversight of auditing services and the accounting complaint process;
2. forces CEOs and CFOs to certify the appropriateness of the financial statements filed with the SEC;

3. makes it unlawful to mislead, coerce, or fraudulently influence an accountant engaged in auditing activities;
4. forces executives of the firm to forfeit any profit from bonus or stock sales resulting in earnings that needed to be restated as a result of misconduct; and
5. prohibits executives from making stock transactions during the time in which the employee pension plan blacks out employee stock transactions.

Enhanced Financial Disclosures

The new law tries to make executive actions more transparent to shareholders. Specifically the Act does the following:

1. requires the disclosure of "off-balance sheet transactions" and corrections in reporting identified by auditors;
2. decreases the time an executive has to report company stock (and other equity) trades to the SEC to two days;
3. prohibits the lending of money by public companies to executives, except for the use of home loans;
4. requires increased internal financial controls and review by the board of directors;
5. encourages a code of ethics for senior officers of the company and report changes and exemptions to the SEC; and
6. requires a financial expert on the board of director's audit committee.

Analysts Conflicts of Interests

The role of securities analysts and their failure to monitor the company is detailed in Chapter 5. In recognizing this failure, the Act tasks the SEC to develop rules for making sure that analysts are separated from investment banking activities and that any conflicts of interests that analysts may have are fully disclosed.

SEC Resources and Authority

One limitation that the SEC has had over the years is that the organization is small compared to the industry it regulates. The SEC regulates tens of thousands of public companies, investment banks, auditors, and other participants in the stock and bond markets. In order to help the SEC expand its monitoring and investigative capabilities, the Act appropriates more money for the SEC and mandates the hiring of at least 200 more employees.

Figure 10.1 shows the annual budget provided to the SEC since 1995. It is clear that the budget remained nearly constant until the outbreak of corporate governance problems in 1999 and 2000. Nevertheless, the SEC budget expanded greatly after the passage of Sarbanes-Oxley.

Corporate and Criminal Fraud, Accountability, and Penalties

To make it easier to prosecute executive criminal behavior in the future, the new law spells out new or altered definitions of criminal behaviors and stiffens penalties. For example, the destruction or falsification of documents in a federal

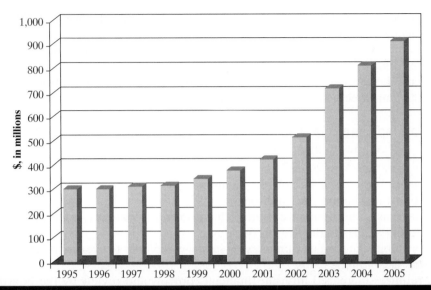

FIGURE 10.1   SEC Annual Budget Authority

investigation or bankruptcy can be punished with a fine and/or imprisonment of up to 10 years. Destruction of audit materials is punishable by a fine and/or imprisonment of up to five years. The statute of limitations for securities fraud is changed to two years after the discovery of the facts or five years after the violation. The bill also protects employee whistle blowers from retaliation by the company or its executives.

The penalties for committing white-collar crimes were generally increased from a maximum of 5 years imprisonment to 20 years in most cases. While this pertains to just the *maximum* prison sentence, federal sentencing guidelines were also amended. That is, the intent is for the actual *average* white-collar prison sentence to increase, not just the maximum. The company CEO, CFO, and Chairman are required to certify the appropriateness of the financial statements. If they willfully violate the integrity of the disclosures, they can be fined up to $1 million and serve up to 10 years in prison.

WILL THE ACT BE BENEFICIAL?

Note that the Sarbanes-Oxley Act addresses many of the problems outlined in this book. For example, the Act addresses problems with auditing, boards of directors, executive behavior, the SEC, and analysts. Thus far, however, it might be fair to say that legal scholars, corporate executives, and, to a lesser extent, large shareholders, have been critical of the Act. In general, legal scholars seem to think that the Act is either misplaced or repetitive to existing laws.[2] For example, aside from giving loans to the executives, they argue that Enron would have complied with the governance rules of Sarbanes-Oxley. Yet that did not inhibit Enron from governance failures that caused it to collapse. In addition, many argue that compliance with the Act is too burdensome and expensive.[3] Companies report that the average expense for implementing the Act was $5.1 million and that the average ongoing annual cost of compliance is $3.7 million.[4]

However, it will probably take some time before the Act can be determined a success or a failure. What will make assessing the Act especially difficult is that we will not know how much fraud would have been committed had the Act not been passed nor will we be able to easily attribute any increase in investor confidence directly to the Act. The latter issue is especially problematic as firms can verifiably know the costs of compliance but they *cannot* reliably associate any increase in the firm's value as a result of the Act. For this reason the Act will probably continue to be a topic of debate for some years.

OTHER REGULATORY CHANGES

In 2002, in light of the burgeoning number of accounting scandals, the SEC Chairman called on the New York Stock Exchange and the NASDAQ Stock Market to take a fresh look at their corporate governance listing standards. The markets were challenged to develop and adopt listing standards to address the crisis in investor confidence. Because they developed new governance standards at that same time as the Sarbanes-Oxley Act was being debated, it is not surprising that their new rules are similar to the Act's laws. However, there are a few differences that reflect the distinctive types of firms listed on the two exchanges. In November 2003, the SEC approved both the NYSE's and the NASDAQ's changes in listing standards.

The New York Stock Exchange

The NYSE can impose rules on NYSE-listed firms only, which means that its rules do not affect non-listed firms, nor can it impose rules on other members of the business community, such as auditors and financial analysts. We focus here on those rules that were adopted by the NYSE but not adopted by the Act.

Most of the new NYSE corporate governance rules have to do with the structure, function, and incentives of the board of directors. Specifically, the NYSE mandates that companies have a *majority of independent directors*. A director is not independent if he (or immediate family) has worked for the company or its auditor within the past five years. The board members that are not also executives of the company *must meet regularly* without the presence of management.

The NYSE also requires specific functions of the board. For example, the *nominating committee of the board must be composed entirely of independent directors* and perform certain duties. This is also true of the compensation committee. Otherwise the executives would have undue influence on their own compensation. The audit committee must also be independent. However, the members of this committee will have an *increased authority and responsibility to hire and fire the auditing firm*. To handle this expanded responsibility, the audit committee members are to have necessary experience and expertise in finance and accounting. To help maintain the independence of audit committee board members, members are not to receive pay from the company outside of their regular director fees, especially consulting fees.

Lastly, the NYSE will require that *shareholders approve all executive equity-based compensation plans.* That is, there will be a shareholder vote on whether the CEO gets a certain number of stock options or restricted stock shares. This rule creates more transparency because each shareholder will receive a proxy statement detailing the compensation proposal.

NASDAQ Stock Market

The firms listing on the NASDAQ Stock Market tend to be smaller, on average, than those listing on the NYSE. The NASDAQ also lists a greater proportion of companies in the technology industry than the NYSE. Therefore, NASDAQ adopted rules in the same spirit as those adopted by the NYSE but with differences intended to fit better with its listing firms.

For example, smaller firms often have a smaller number of board members. The Sarbanes-Oxley Act and the new NYSE rules empower independent directors and give them much responsibility. However, the implementation may overwhelm a small number of independent directors serving on a small firm board. Consider a board with only seven directors. Only four independent board members are needed to create a board with an independent director majority. However, having only four independent directors makes it difficult to have independent committees for executive compensation, nomination, auditing, etc. So instead of having a rule that an independent compensation committee must approve the executive's compensation, they provide an alternative that the independent directors can approve the compensation directly (without being all members of a compensation committee).

While the NYSE requires that shareholders approve all executive equity-based compensation plans, the NASDAQ recognizes that offering "inducement" options to new employees are a common and important practice in the technology sector. The NASDAQ rules allow these offers to new employees without shareholder approval if they are approved by a majority of independent directors and properly disclosed.

Only international firms listing on NASDAQ can apply for a waiver from corporate governance rules that would be contrary to the firm's home country law or business practice. In those cases where a waiver is appropriate, it must be disclosed in annual SEC filings.

CAUSES OF SECURITIES REGULATIONS: A HISTORY LESSON

It is obvious that the corporate and investment community scandals and the market downturn of 2000 and 2001 is what led to the enactment of the Sarbanes-Oxley Act. The U.S. government actually has a history of being reactive rather than proactive when it comes to its laws regarding the investment industry. In general, the government has responded with new and tighter regulations and laws in the face of two types of occurrences: major bear markets and/or scandalous periods. Consider the securities laws shown in Example 10.1. The securities acts passed in 1933 and 1934 followed the corporate governance

EXAMPLE 10.1

MAJOR LAWS CREATED TO PROTECT INVESTORS

Act	*Purpose*	*Preceded by*
1933 and 1934 Banking Act (Glass-Steagall Act) and Securities Exchange Act	Separates commercial and investment banking creates SEC as market regulators	Corporate and investment community scandals and stock market crash of 1929 and ensuing bear market removes nearly 90% of Dow value
1940 Investment Company Act and Investment Advisors Act	Regulates investment companies and advisors	Market decline of 25% from October 1939 to May 1940
1970 Securities Investor Protection Act	Creates Securities Investor Protection Corporation and insurance from broker defaults	Market decline of 30% from April 1969 to June 1970
1974 Employee Retirement Income Security Act	Regulates pension funds	Long bear market from December 1972 to September 1974 takes the Dow down 40%
1988 Insider Trading and Securities Fraud Enforcement Act	Increases penalties and liabilities for insider trading and fraudulent activities	Stock market crash of 1987 takes Dow down by more than 40%
2002 Public Company Accounting Reform and Investor Protection Act	Increases regulation of auditors, lengthens punishment for white-collar crimes, and creates more corporate fraud laws	Corporate and investment community scandals and $2\frac{1}{2}$ year bear market reduced Dow by 35%, NASDAQ declines 75%

problems of the late 1920s, the 1929 stock market crash, and the beginning of the Great Depression. The investment company and advisors acts in 1940 followed a bear market that experienced a 25 percent downturn in the stock market. The creations of the Securities Investor Protection Corporation (SIPC) in 1970 followed a bear market in the late 1960s, which saw a 30 percent decline in the stock market. Investor protection laws also followed the bear market of the early 1970s. Note that the enactment of the 1988 laws immediately followed the market crash of October 19, 1987. And of course, the 2002 Public Company Accounting Reform and Investor Protection Act followed the recent corporate scandals and severe stock market decline in 2000 and 2001.

Likewise, securities laws have often been repealed during times of economic strength and stock market euphoria. The 1920s and the 1990s share similarities. Both decades experienced strong economic expansions and strong bull markets. In the middle (or toward the end) of the excitement over stocks during both of these periods, the government relaxed its laws that protected investors.

Consider the examples in Example 10.2. In 1927, the stock market was toward the end of a bull market that had increased values by over 200 percent. There were many new companies conducting IPOs that were not yet stable enough to be offered to investors. Investors did not seem to care and rushed in to snap them up. The commercial banks were prevented from getting into the investment banking activities to share in the lucrative fees of underwriting IPOs. They lobbied the government to change the rules and succeeded. Commercial banks began helping companies issue securities such as IPOs. Unfortunately the stock market crash of 1929 left commercial banks with many losses that jeopardized people's bank deposits. Of course, this led to the enactment of 1933 Banking Act discussed in Example 10.1.

Now lets examine the three law changes in the 1990s. The Private Securities Litigation Reform Act limited the ability of investors to sue companies and executives for damages due to corporate fraud in federal courts. This law was enacted in the midst of a strong bull market that increased the value of the Dow Jones Industrial Average by 60 percent. It was followed three years later with a similar act that applied to state courts. Perhaps what is most telling is the enactment of the Financial Services Modernization Act in 1999. It allowed commercial banks to associate themselves with investment banks again, similar to the 1927 capitulation. Again, this reduction in investor protection occurred toward the end of a market rally that increased the Dow by 125 percent.

While it may seem natural to enact laws to fix bad times and loosen laws to enjoy good times, does such a policy make sense? One could argue that securities regulations and laws should protect investors regardless of the economic and stock market conditions. If the Sarbanes-Oxley Act was created simply as a reaction to bad times then its effectiveness for the long run may be questionable, especially if there is a chance that some parts of it will be

EXAMPLE 10.2

REPEALS OF SOME INVESTOR PROTECTIONS

Acts	*Purpose*	*Preceded by*
1927 Government agency policy allowing commercial banks to issue securities	Allows commercial banks into investment banking activities	Stock market rose over 200% from 1925 to 1928
1995 Private Securities Litigation Reform Act	Limits the ability and available damages of investors suing for corporate fraud	Dow increased 60% between 1993 and 1995
1998 Securities Litigation Uniform Standards Act	Precludes plaintiffs from bringing securities actions in state courts	Dow increased 125% from 1996 to 1999
1999 Financial Services Modernization Act	Allows the combining of commercial and investment banking activities	Dow increased 125% from 1996 to 1999

repealed in the future during a market upturn. A loosening of securities regulations during a bull market may lead to a bubble market. If a bubble occurs a crash will inevitably follow. This could lead to more scandals and more investor protection laws. So securities regulations are cyclical. Is it good to have such a cycle?

INTERNATIONAL PERSPECTIVE

While corporate scandals were front-page news in the U.S. and the U.S. Congress was debating the Sarbanes-Oxley Act and countries all over the world were also examining their own corporate governance policies. These actions were also motivated by their own corporate scandals, such as Royal Ahold (of The Netherlands), Parmalat (of Italy), Daewoo Group (of South Korea), Vivendi Universal (of France), and Adecco (a Swiss firm), to name few. Example 10.3 shows the principle outcomes of these efforts for various countries.[5]

EXAMPLE 10.3

WORLDWIDE FOCUS ON CORPORATE GOVERNANCE

Country	*Law or Recommendation*	*Date*
Australia	Principles of Good Corporate Governance and Best Practice Recommendations	March 2003
Austria	Austrian Code of Corporate Governance	November 2002, updated April 2005
Belgium	Belgian Corporate Governance Code	December 2004
Brazil	Code of Best Practice of Corporate Governance	March 2004
Canada	National Policy 58–201 Corporate Governance Guidelines	December 2003
China	The Code of Corporate Governance for Listed Companies in China	January 2001
Denmark	Revised Recommendations for Corporate Governance in Denmark	August 2005
Finland	Corporate Governance Recommendations for Listed Companies	December 2003
France	The Corporate Governance of Listed Corporations	October 2003
Germany	The German Corporate Governance Code (The Cromme Code)	February 2002, amended May 2003
Greece	Principles of Corporate Governance	July 2001
Hong Kong	Hong Kong Code on Corporate Governance	November 2004
Italy	Corporate Governance Code (il Codice di Autodisciplina delle società quotate rivisitato)	July 2002
Japan	Principles of Corporate Governance for Listed Companies	April 2004

Netherlands	The Dutch corporate governance code	December 2003
Norway	The Norwegian Code of Practice for Corporate Governance	December 2004
Portugal	Recommendations on Corporate Governance	November 2003
Russia	The Russian Code of Corporate Conduct	April 2002
South Korea	Code of Best Practice for Corporate Governance	September 1999
Sweden	Swedish Code of Corporate Governance *Report of the Code Group*	December 2004
Switzerland	Swiss Code of Best Practice for Corporate Governance	June 2002
Taiwan	Taiwan Corporate Governance Best-Practice Principles	2002
Thailand	Code of Best Practice for Directors of Listed Companies	October 2002
Turkey	Corporate Governance Principles	June 2003
United Kingdom	The Combined Code on Corporate Governance	July 2003

In the U.S., securities laws are made by the legislative branch of the government and enforcement is left to the SEC (see Chapter 9). As noted above, rules can also be created by private organizations, such as the NYSE and NASDAQ. The laws enacted by governments can be enforced by punishments through criminal penalties and civil fines. However, most countries have not formally laid down full, detailed corporate governance provisions in the law itself. The legal status of governance codes varies dramatically between countries.[6]

In several European countries, the codes have the status of mere recommendations, drawn up by professional associations and academics without the explicit support of the government (such as Italy and France). Implementation of these codes is voluntary and its enforcement is based on the assessment by market forces. In some cases enforcement may be based on the rules of a business association supporting the code.

Sometimes these private bodies and commissions do have the support of the government. In the Netherlands and Germany, recommended codes have become *de facto* law when governments made explicit reference to it, hence attaching express legal consequences. The debate in these countries has focused on the remedies and sanctions for enforcing the code and the consequences of this hybrid of public and private law are still being debated. In other countries, corporate governance code is created by the stock exchange. In these cases, the code may take the form of a recommendation or may even be formulated as a listing condition. In the case of the U.K., the Combined Code applies to listed companies.

Summary

In response to the corporate and investment community scandals during 2000 and 2001, the U.S. government responded with the enactment of the Sarbanes-Oxley Act, otherwise known as the Public Company Accounting Reform and Investor Protection Act of 2002. The Act establishes a non-profit corporation to oversee the audit of public companies, tries to ensure auditor independence, attempts to increase the monitoring ability and responsibilities of boards of directors, tries to make executive actions more transparent to shareholders, tasks the SEC to develop rules for making sure that analysts are separated from investment banking activities, appropriates more money for the SEC, and spells out new or altered definitions of criminal behaviors and stiffens penalties. Will the Act be beneficial? Time will tell. However, there are already legal scholars, business executives, and even large shareholders who are already critical of the Act.

Other regulatory changes also took place in 2002. Both the NYSE and NASDAQ developed and adopted listing standards to address the crisis in investor confidence. Most of the new NYSE corporate governance rules deal with the structure, function, and incentives of the board of directors. NASDAQ adopted rules in the same spirit as those adopted by the NYSE.

It is common for the U.S. government to respond with new and tighter securities regulations during or after market downturns and/or scandalous periods. The Sarbanes-Oxley Act is one example but there are other examples as well. When regulations are created to fix bad times and relaxed to enjoy good times then it causes a tendency for cyclical behavior. Further, when regulations are just responses to economic conditions, it may raise questions as to whether or not these regulations are best for society in the long-run.

WEB Info about New Governance Rules

SEC, Proposed and Final Rules
www.sec.gov/rules.shtml

Public Company Accounting Oversight Board
www.pcaobus.org/

NYSE Corporate Governance Listing Standards
www.nyse.com/about/listed/1101074746736.html

European Corporate Governance Institute, Index of Codes
www.ecgi.org/codes/all_codes.php

Review Questions

1. Describe the major components of the Sarbanes-Oxley Act.
2. Describe the major components of the new NYSE regulations.
3. What leads to new securities regulations in the U.S.?

Discussion Questions

1. As a current or future shareholder, are you happy with the Sarbanes-Oxley Act? As a current or future business employee, are you happy with the Act? What has been the general consensus of the Sarbanes-Oxley Act among your colleagues at work, your friends, and in the media?
2. Which parts of the Act do you think were good ideas? Which parts do you think were bad ideas? Which parts of the Act do you think will work? Which parts do you think will be repealed in the future?
3. In your opinion, what weaknesses or flaws of the corporate governance system are *not* addressed in the Act?
4. Do you think it is problematic to strengthen and relax securities laws depending on market conditions? First, argue that it is a problem. Then, argue that it is not a problem.

Exercises

1. Do some research and identify the primary complaints that executives have with the Sarbanes-Oxley Act. Are others complaining about it too? Try to explain why or why not.
2. Find the opinions of three legal scholars and describe their assessment of the Sarbanes-Oxley Act. Find a dissenting opinion from another legal scholar and describe it.
3. Go to the ecgi.org website. This site contains a link to corporate governance codes from countries all over the world. Provide some thoughts on codes from 3 *distinct* countries and try to explain why there might be differences among the codes.
4. Do some research and provide a progress report on the new NYSE and NASDAQ regulations.
5. Do some research and try to find out whether or not firms are reluctant to list on the NYSE because of it's new regulations? What about international listings on the NYSE? Have international listings increased or decreased since the passage of NYSE's new regulations? Some people predict that it might increase. Why do you think that they are predicting this?

Exercises for Non-U.S. Students

1. Describe your country's corporate code or laws with regard to corporate governance. Also, in your opinion, what are its strengths and weaknesses? Finally, what do you think caused the code or laws to be strong or weak?
2. Identify all Sarbanes-Oxley rules that your country also has and identify those Sarbanes-Oxley rules that your country does not have. Why does your country have and not have these specific rules?
3. Find out the listing requirements for your country's major stock exchange. What kinds of corporate governance rules does it have? Provide an assessment of these rules.

Endnotes

1. For example, see Stuart Banner, "What Causes New Securities Regulation? 300 Years of Evidence," *Washington University Law Quarterly* 75, no. 2 (1997): 849–850.

2. Of course, it's difficult to summarize all of the legal literature that has come out against Sarbanes-Oxley, but the interested reader can refer to Roberta Romano, "The Sarbanes-Oxley Act and the Making of Quack Corporate Governance," NYU, Law and Econ Research Paper 04–032; Yale Law & Econ Research Paper 297; Yale ICF Working Paper 04–37; ECGI—Finance Working Paper 52/2004, September 26, 2004, for a thorough overview.

3. In a *Business Week* article, it estimates that compliance to the Act can be as high as $35 million annually for large firms ("Death, Taxes, and Sarbanes-Oxley?" *Business Week*, January 17, 2005).

4. 31st Annual Board of Directors Study, Korn/Ferry International, (Los Angeles, CA, 2004).

5. These laws and recommendations were obtained from European Corporate Governance Institute's website on Codes & Principles, *www.ecgi.org/codes/index.php*.

6. See Eddy Wymeersch, "Enforcement of Corporate Governance Codes" (June 2005), ECGI—Law Working Paper No. 46/2005.

CHAPTER

11

CORPORATE CITIZENSHIP

The previous chapters discuss corporate governance from the perspective of agency theory. As described in the first chapter, agency theory focuses on the separation of ownership and control. Shareholders (owners) are the central point of concern. From this perspective, corporate governance is mainly about the incentive systems and monitors designed to protect shareholder interests. The primary goal of the firm is to create wealth for these shareholders.

However, this is not the only perspective from which to consider corporate governance. Many believe that companies should have a greater responsibility to society. Proponents argue that companies have unique opportunities to improve society. This *stakeholder* view of the firm describes the firm as having many different groups with legitimate interests in the firm's activities. Corporate governance is then defined as the mechanisms that ensure corporations take responsibility for directing their activities in a manner fair to all stakeholders. Strategic management concepts argue that this is based on creating positive relationships with stakeholders. Through creating these positive relationships, firms can create sustainable economic wealth.

In particular, agency theory has been an important perspective for formulating governance rules, laws, and policy in the U.S. However, many other countries have operated under the idea that large corporations have a greater responsibility in society than just maximizing shareholder wealth. Their governance rules tend to be influenced to a greater extent by this duty to an expanded set of stakeholders.

If U.S. firms believed they had a social obligation to be good citizens then this sense of responsibility for the greater good could serve as yet another governance device. However, do firms have a sense of social responsibility? Some might say that they do not but others may argue that they should. We discuss the stakeholder view of the firm and we also describe problems with the view, which make it difficult to use this view to ensure good governance.

STAKEHOLDER VIEW OF THE FIRM

A company must maintain relationships with several groups that affect or are affected by its decisions.[1] Stakeholders are identified as people or groups with legitimate interests in various aspects of the company's activities. Note that stakeholders are defined by their interest in the corporation, not whether the corporation has any interest in them. Companies have varying responsibilities to each of their stakeholders. While some relationships may be more valuable (or important) than others, no one group should be able to dominate all of the others. These relationships between managers and stakeholders are based on a moral or ethical foundation.

Clearly groups, such as stockholders, employees, and creditors have a strong interest in the firm. But what other groups might be considered stakeholders? Figure 11.1 shows the different types of groups that might be considered stakeholders of the firm. The primary stakeholders (sometimes called contractual stakeholders) have direct, contractually determined relationships. While the stockholder is considered a very important stakeholder, other groups are also important. Company employees have short-term interests in the firm in the form of pay and working conditions and long-term interests in the form of pension and health care. Employees often have labor unions to manage their relationship with the firm. Creditors, customers, and suppliers also have legitimate interests in the organization. The secondary (or diffuse) stakeholders are impacted by the firm's actions but have limited contractual connection to it. Examples of secondary stakeholders may be its competitors and environmental activists. Certainly, local communities, governments, and all of society may be affected by the company's decisions.

The figure shows just one way to categorize the different stakeholders of a firm. Other distinctions could be made. For example, groupings can be based on the various activities of the firm and those that they impact. It can be based on

FIGURE 11.1   Company Stakeholders

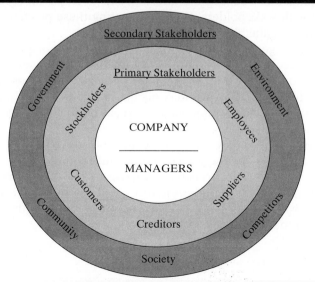

a resource-view, or industry structure, or by social and political affiliations. Or these stakeholders can be grouped by institutional, economic, and ethical interests. There is no consensus on how these stakeholders should be categorized. However, all the stakeholder views illustrate a much different perspective than agency theory — companies have responsibilities to groups other than to stockholders.

A stakeholder view of the firm places its executives at the center of managing relations with each stakeholder group. The managerial objective in this view is to maximize sustainable organizational wealth (all stakeholders' utilities) by optimizing these relationships. Many companies now have an organizational unit tasked with communicating with stakeholders. These units may have camouflaged names like "corporate communication department" or "public affairs department." Others use more direct names like "sustainability group" or "corporate social responsibility committee."

EXAMPLE 11.1

WAL-MART'S BATTLE WITH STAKEHOLDERS

Wal-Mart operates over 3,500 discount stores in the U.S. (Wal-Mart, Super Centers, and Sam's Clubs). The firm generates over $10 billion in profits per year. The company is the largest corporate employer in the U.S., with 1.3 million employees, and plans to open about 300 new stores every year.

But Wal-Mart seems to be coming under increasing pressure from different social groups for its business practices. Coalitions of community groups have worked to keep Wal-Mart from coming to their towns. Hundreds of communities have been successful. A recent class-action lawsuit was filed against Wal-Mart on behalf of female employees, arguing that they were being paid less then their male counterparts. Many politicians have noticed that a large portion of Wal-Mart's employees end up on public health care assistance. The firm has endured allegations of child labor law violations, the hiring of illegal immigrants, and violations of worker rights.

Wal-Mart's view is much different. It claims that its low prices help everyone in the community. Also by giving $170 million to charity last year, it is the largest corporate cash contributor in the U.S. Wal-Mart targets 90 percent of its charitable contributions at the local level where Wal-Mart customers and associates live and work.

Whether Wal-Mart has been a good corporate citizen or not is being actively debated. However, one thing seems obvious — Wal-Mart has done a poor job of actively engaging many of its stakeholders to optimize their mutual interests. Having adversarial relationships with employees, potential customers, politicians, and civil rights activists do not seem like wise business choices.

Legal Foundations

The legal underpinnings of the stakeholder view of the firm stems from property rights. This may seem ironic because it is the stockholders who own the firm. If stockholders are the owners, do not they have the property rights? Not necessarily. The definition of property can be expressed as a "bundle" of rights, which may be limited.[2] Owners of property have the right to engage in a limited set of activities.

Consider a land-owner. Building a home requires a building permit. The government agency that grants the permit must first approve the building plans. The building must meet adequate safety and appearance criteria. Land is also zoned for specific uses. These laws and procedures protect citizens that may go on the property (safety) and the landowners in the area (appearance and use). Although they are not owners of the land, these citizens and nearby property owners are stakeholders of this land. They also have rights.

The U.S. government, various state governments, and courts have formalized the rights of stakeholders in corporations. Many states have adopted statues that extend the concern of corporate boards beyond that of the shareholders to other stakeholders, such as employees, creditors, suppliers, customers, and communities. The determination of which rights are held by the corporation (and its owners) and which rights belong to various stakeholders, continues to evolve.

Corporate Social Responsibility

The modern evolution of the stakeholder view of the firm advocates that management develop specific relationships with stakeholder groups. Proponents of this view argue that companies have a social obligation to operate in ethically, socially, and environmentally responsible ways. This active approach is referred to as corporate social responsibility[3] (CSR) or corporate citizenship.

What is a company's responsibility to society? Archie Carroll has offered a four-part taxonomy of CSR that lends itself to corporate citizenship from a managerial perspective. A firm should conduct its business in a manner that meets its economic, legal, ethical, and philanthropy expectations:[4]

Level I: Economic—the first and foremost social responsibility of a firm is economic. The firm must survive by producing goods and services at a profit.

Level II: Legal—society expects firms to operate their business within the legal framework.

Level III: Ethical—these responsibilities are those over and above the ones codified in laws and are in line with societal norms and customs. They are expected, though not required, by society even though they may be ill defined. This could include things such as environmental ethics.

Level IV: Philanthropy—corporate giving is discretionary, although increasingly desired by stakeholder communities.

The economic responsibilities (Level I) have the highest priority. A firm must be efficient and survive over the long term, in order to be useful to society.

However, it must execute its business activities in a legal (Level II) and ethical (Level III) way. Philanthropy (Level IV) is the least important priority. Reconsider the Wal-Mart example through this model of CSR. CSR proponents might argue that any failure of Wal-Mart in higher priority responsibilities, such as legal and ethical considerations, cannot be to offset through greater participation in lower priority responsibilities, such as corporate giving.

While corporate citizenship might include charity or philanthropy (Level IV), the concept focuses more on engagement with stakeholders to achieve mutual goals (Level II and Level III). Proponents of CSR argue that the main drivers of the citizenship trend include the following:

- Globalization, the worldwide expansion of business and market economies;
- Greater power of global firms should fill the activities formerly left to governments;
- Pressure from assertive social activists;
- An increasingly popular environmental movement; and
- A rising desire in the capital markets to punish firms not meeting ethical standards.

Some corporations have responded to this trend by including CSR-oriented statements in their corporate values and goals. These statements recognize that CSR has value in a code of conduct or ethics, a commitment to local communities, an interest in employee health and education, an environmental consciousness, and recognition of social issues (e.g. diversity, social fairness, etc.).

By embracing citizenship goals, advocates claim corporations will insulate themselves from many activist actions, establish stakeholder confidence in management, enhance the firm's reputation, and demonstrate an emphasis on prevention rather than corrective actions.[5] As a result of these perceptions, firms may find that their goodwill opens doors to new communities and additional sales.

However, social responsibility is a dynamic process. It stems from the making of decisions balancing the interests of all stakeholders. But these decisions can only be made from an ongoing conversation among affected parties. For this to occur over time, social awareness must become an integral part of the corporate culture. Ethical considerations become central to this process.

When Enron executives were falsifying revenue and taking excessive risks, they not only hurt their shareholders but other stakeholders as well. Enron hurt their customers who now have to find other vendors, suppliers who depended on Enron's orders, employees who could have worked elsewhere, and the future local economy as current and future jobs have now been taken away. In addition, because the government spent millions investigating and prosecuting Enron executives, society as a whole is harmed as well, as that money could have been spent elsewhere for a greater good. For these Enron executives, where was their sense of corporate citizenship? Can citizenship, or a sense of corporate responsibility to society, be considered a type of monitor?

EXAMPLE 11.2

CORPORATE CITIZENSHIP AT AMERICAN EXPRESS

American Express is the world's largest travel agency and a large issuer of credit cards. It has a presence in 160 countries and more than 40 percent of its 84,000 employees work outside the U.S. The firm has had "company values" long before the term became vogue. American Express values:[6]

- Developing relationships that make a positive difference in their customers' lives;

- Providing outstanding products and unsurpassed service;

- Upholding the highest standards of integrity in all actions;

- Working together across boundaries, to meet the needs of their customers and to help the company win;

- Valuing employees, encouraging their development, and rewarding their performance;

- Being citizens in the communities in which employees live and work;

- Exhibiting a strong will to win in the marketplace and in every aspect of the business;

- Being personally accountable for delivering on commitments.

Note that only three of the eight values can be clearly identified as relating to the business bottom-line of the firm. Many of these values are clearly grounded in moral and social objectives.

These values are far more than just statements for the company coffee mug. American Express ensures that these values become an integral part of mainstream operations by surveying each employee on how the company has performed with respect to these values. The results of this survey are then used as one of several measurements used to determine compensation issues of managers. Social goals can really only be effective in the long run when objectives can be measured and when progress success or failure is tied to managerial compensation.

GOVERNANCE AND STAKEHOLDER THEORY

Can stakeholder theory play a role in corporate governance? In the agency theory view of the firm, governance is about aligning managerial incentives and providing monitoring of management behavior. In the stakeholder view of the firm, how can management be forced to internalize the welfare of stakeholders?

Managerial incentives can be provided by rewarding management on the basis of some measure of the welfare of the stakeholders.[7] This process requires clear objectives and performance measurements. Defining acceptable, multiple missions suitable to all stakeholder groups can be tricky. Another key problem to be overcome is whether a measure of stakeholder welfare is available. It is harder to measure the firm's performance to its employees, customers, etc., than to stockhold-ers. There is no *accounting* measure (like earnings) or *market* value measure (like stock price) of the impact of past and current managerial decisions on stakeholder welfare. The result is that aligning managerial incentives with multiple stakeholder groups and measuring overall performance can become a noisy and chaotic process.

To date, there is no consensus on how to measure and report on changes in stakeholder welfare. Ideas that have supporters are the Balanced Scorecard[8] approach and the "triple bottom line."[9] The Balanced Scorecard measures performance in four perspectives: customer, internal processes, employee learn-ing and growth, and financial success. Triple bottom line accounting expands the traditional company-reporting framework to take into account financial, environmental, and social outcomes. While both systems are used by some companies, neither has been generally adopted.

Regardless of the overall measurement of outcomes, organizational theory states that the firm will only value CSR goals if the company executive exhibits strong leadership in instilling corporate responsibility within the company's culture. The values of the culture influence the processes by which the company will try to solve a problem.[10] Executives signal which values are important through both employee incentives and through organizational structure.[11] The primary means is that of setting the criteria for recruitment and promotion. CSR goals are best executed when individual employees have promotion criteria incentives tied to those goals. A secondary means are the design of organizational structure and procedures that are aligned with the values. Mission statements, which reflect CSR goals and organizational units tasked with interacting with stakeholders, are examples of structural means of promoting culture values. The values set at the top of the company filter down throughout the organization. Therefore leadership in corporate responsibility is critical to its adoption by a firm.

CRITICISMS

The authors, researchers, and practitioners of the stakeholder view of the firm use the concepts in different ways and often use contradictory evidence and argu-ments to support the theory. For example, some characterize stakeholder theory as a **descriptive theory**. It is used to describe what firms are doing and how they are doing it. Others use stakeholder theory from an **instrumental perspective**. This approach provides principles and practices that should be implemented to achieve (or avoid) certain results. They portent that if corporate performance results A, B, and C are desired, then the firm should implement standards and practices X, Y, and Z. Lastly, the stakeholder view is used to advocate how firms should behave based on ethical and philosophical principles. Advocates of corpo-rate social responsibility or corporate citizenship use this **normative approach**.

Is the stakeholder view correct? Should we view firms from a stakeholder perspective? If so, then how can we operationalize it? Because the stakeholder view is not a well-defined theory, it is difficult to assess. As an example, consider one of the primary stakeholders, employees. Providing employees with high quality health care seems consistent with the tenets of the stakeholder view of the firm. The descriptive approach might ask how many companies are providing quality health care. The instrumental approach would be interested in how the providing of quality health care impacts the firm's stock returns and operating performance. The normative approach advocates that firms should provide quality health care because it is the moral thing to do. However, none of these provide the chance to accept or reject the validity of the stakeholder view.

Since the stakeholder view of the firm is difficult to empirically validate or reject, can it be philosophically criticized? Even critics of corporate citizenship agree that companies should act responsibly and should be seen doing so. After all, this is often good for business. However, that is different than aggressively pursuing the corporate social responsibility doctrine advocated today. Indeed, critics argue that deviating too far from the profit-maximizing role of companies would be harmful to society.

The critics' argument stems from the experience that economic progress comes from profit-related activities. The primary role of business in society is to act as a vehicle for economic development. In a market-oriented economic system, economic progress results from entrepreneurial opportunities and competitive pressures. Successfully introduced new or improved products enhance profits while increasing the quality of life in society. Competition forces business to continually work to provide goods and services more effectively and more efficiently.

When managers have to take into account a wider range of goals and involve themselves in stakeholder engagement activities, higher costs and impaired business performance is likely to follow. When trying to serve "many masters," managers often become ineffective in achieving any of the goals.[12] Indeed, more exacting environmental and social standards will bring more regulation. Over-regulation exacts an enormous cost on society in the form of limiting competition, narrowing opportunities, and worsening economic performance. History shows that when the economy is intentionally focused on social goals, such as employment, production, etc., society becomes worse off. The poor economic performance of the former Soviet Union, Cuba, and China (before its more recent move toward a market-based economy) shows this.

EXAMPLE 11.3

DOW JONES STOXX SUSTAINABILITY INDEX

One way to measure the success of firms engaged in corporate citizenship activities is to form a stock index of such firms. The SAM Group measures a company's "corporate sustainability" and forms an index of the best companies (in cooperation with Dow Jones Indexes and STOXX Limited).

The SAM Group purports that "Corporate sustainability is a business approach that creates long-term shareholder value by embracing opportunities and managing risks deriving from economic, environmental, and social developments." Specifically SAM quantifies the quality of a company's strategy and management in dealing with economic, environmental, and social opportunities. Competence is measured in areas such as strategy, financial performance, customer relationships, stakeholder engagement, governance standards, and employee satisfaction.

The Dow Jones STOXX 600 Index is designed to provide a broad representation of the European market, by including 600 firms from Austria, Belgium, Denmark, Finland, France, Germany, Greece, Ireland, Italy, Luxembourg, the Netherlands, Norway, Portugal, Spain, Sweden, Switzerland, and the U.K. The narrower Dow Jones STOXX Sustainability Index (DJSI) tracks the performance of the top 20 percent (in terms of sustainability) of the companies in the Dow Jones STOXX 600 Index. This index started at the beginning of 1999. As of August 31, 2005, the DJSI STOXX included 160 companies.

Figure 11.2 shows both the DJ STOXX Index and the DJSI[13] since the creation of the DJSI. The DJ STOXX Index is scaled to 100 on January 1, 1999 to equal the DJSI. Notice that performance of both indexes is nearly identical. In late 2001 and 2002, the sustainability index seems to be higher than the broader index. However, this reverses in 2004. This evidence does not seem to support the argument of corporate citizenship critics that companies serving multiple masters often become ineffective at achieving any of the goals. Neither does the evidence support proponents argument that corporate citizenship maximizes company wealth. The sustainability index performs no better than the broader index.

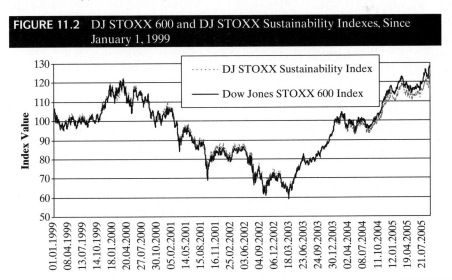

FIGURE 11.2   DJ STOXX 600 and DJ STOXX Sustainability Indexes, Since January 1, 1999

INTERNATIONAL PERSPECTIVES

Corporate citizenship has different historical roots in different regions of the world and therefore is viewed with different perspectives. For example, CSR in the U.S. derived from the conflict between stockholder-focused managers and social activists. This unenthusiastic relationship between companies and some activist groups created a negative attitude toward stakeholder theory in the business community. Over the past few decades, many U.S. business groups have slowly began to embrace CSR ideas. In the U.K. and Europe, corporate citizenship has been viewed less negatively and is currently a more holistic concept. In India, the lack of government efficacy in the provision of social welfare has caused corporations to step into the role of helping society. Stakeholder concern is integrated within the firm and is based on family values.

A stakeholder view of the firm is also reflected in many laws internationally. In the U.K., company directors are mandated to include the interests of employees in decision making (Companies Act). In Germany, employee representation is required on one of the two-tier boards (co-determination laws). The European Union permits corporations to take into account the interests of employees, creditors, customers, and potential investors (harmonization laws). In Japan, after the World War II, corporations were tasked with the responsibility for rebuilding the Japanese economy. The same was true for Korea after its Korean War in the 1950s. Korean companies that focused on exporting were even given tax breaks to help them bring capital into Korea.

How actively are managers engaging stakeholders? This is a difficult question to assess. The Conference Board surveyed over 700 companies on the issues of corporate citizenship between 2000 and 2001.[14] The firms tended to be very large (over 95 percent of the firms surveyed recorded over $1 billion in sales annually). The companies that respond to such surveys are those that have a positive attitude toward corporate citizenship. Instead of declaring a negative attitude, managers that do not value CSR simply do not complete the survey. Therefore we should consider the survey responses as a survey of firms actively engaged in CSR.

In the surveys, CEOs were asked what their firm's role would play in creating good business and good society. They were given the choices of being a leader, a partner, or a supporter. Results are shown in Figure 11.3 by geographical region for the companies completing the survey. Note that the most frequent answer from U.S. managers was to be a leader. European managers and those in the Asia-Pacific region most often chose to be partners. In general, managers from Europe and Asia-Pacific generally believed that the government should assume the leadership role in designing social good standards and activities.

The surveys also asked managers about how effective they were in implementing standards, codes, and programs that will result in achieving their corporate citizenship goals. Figure 11.4 shows that these companies believe they still have much room for improvement. Keep in mind, however, that it is more difficult to achieve higher standard goals than lower goals. Nevertheless, there seems to be a large difference between U.S. and European firms and those in Asia-Pacific. Over 50 percent

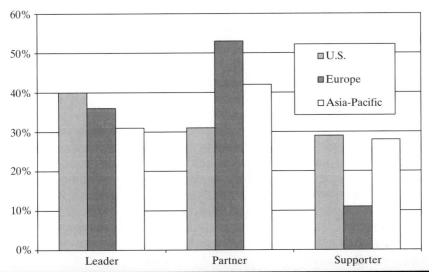

FIGURE 11.3   What Role Will Your Company Play Increasing Good Business and Good Society?

Data Source: Corporate Citizenship in the New Century: Accountability, Transparency, and Global Stakeholder Engagement, The Conference Board. Research Report # R-1314-02-RR. July 2002.

FIGURE 11.4   How Effective are Your Efforts Today to Address the Citizenship Factors that Will Assure Your Success Tomorrow?

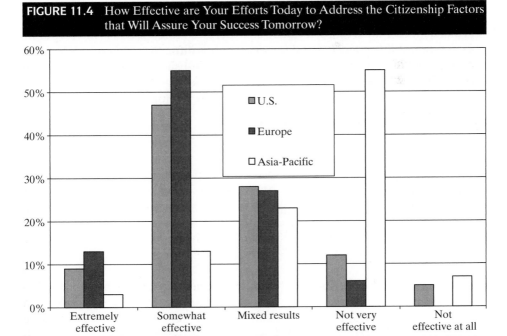

Data Source: Corporate Citizenship in the New Century: Accountability, Transparency, and Global Stakeholder Engagement, The Conference Board. Research Report # R-1314-02-RR. July 2002.

of the firms from the U.S. and Europe responded as being either extremely effective or somewhat effective in their efforts. Only 20 percent of the Asia-Pacific firms believed they were so effective. Any lack of effectiveness may arise from not having a structured program to engage stakeholders on a regular basis. Only 60 percent of the responding firms have a structured program. Nevertheless, many companies are learning how to deal with this new area of corporate accountability.

Summary

The stakeholder view of the firm does not focus on the maximization of shareholder wealth but rather an optimization of the sustainable economic wealth of all stakeholders. Stockholders, employees, customers, communities, and the environment are just some examples of stakeholders. Their legitimate interest in the firm arises from the perspective that these stakeholders have property rights in the firm. Corporate stakeholder relationships have different historical roots in different regions of the world and therefore are viewed with different perspectives.

The modern evolution of the stakeholder view of the firm, called corporate social responsibility or corporate citizenship, advocates that companies have a social obligation to operate in ethically, socially, and environmentally responsible ways. By embracing citizenship goals, corporations may insulate themselves from activist actions, enhance the firm's reputation, and find that their goodwill opens doors to new communities and additional sales. Therefore, a sense of corporate citizenship potentially represents another way to affect business people's behaviors and actions. In this sense, it can be considered a monitor. But is the corporate social responsibility concept good for society? It is difficult to do well while doing good. A company can fail in its social goals and still succeed as a business but it cannot fail as a business and still succeed in its social goals. In addition, how do we create a governance system based on this sense of citizenship?

WEB Info about Corporate Citizenship

The Conference Board
www.conference-board.org

CSR Europe
www.csreurope.org

The Corporate Citizenship Company
www.corporate-citizenship.co.uk

Review Questions

1. Name and describe as many stakeholders of the corporation as you can.
2. Describe the differences between agency theory and stakeholder theory.
3. Name and describe the four levels of corporate social responsibility.
4. What are the criticisms of a profit-maximization focus?
5. What are the criticisms of the stakeholder view of the firm?

Discussion Questions

1. Do you think corporations should have a responsibility to society in general? Explain.
2. Lets say companies should be good citizens. How can this be measured? How can it be enforced?

3. How should we solve a stakeholder crisis? Who would be the monitors? Who should be the monitors? What regulations can be imposed?

Exercises

1. Report on the latest developments of CSR as described by The Conference Board (*www.conference-board.org*).
2. Go to *www.wakeupwalmart.com*. Describe the current stakeholder problems with Wal-Mart. Also go to *www.walmart.com* and determine what Wal-Mart is doing to engage the stakeholders.

3. How might corporations engage environmental activists in a productive and legal way?
4. Investigate and report on the standards of corporate social responsibility issued by the Social Venture Network (*www.svn.org*).

Exercises for Non-U.S. Students

1. Does your country subscribe to an agency view or the stakeholder view of the firm? Explain.
2. In what ways are firms in your country viewed differently from U.S. firms? Are they seen as contributors to the national economy? Are corporate executives looked upon as greedy or as important social leaders?
3. What is your overall opinion of the role of your country's firms in your country? Is it good for the long run? What criteria (profits, environment, etc.) should be applied?

Endnotes

1. An early organization of the stakeholder theory concepts is provided in E. R. Freeman, *Strategic Management: A Stakeholder Approach*, Pitman, Boston, MA, 1984.
2. Thomas Donaldson and Lee E. Preston, "The Stakeholder Theory of the Corporation: Concepts, Evidence, and Implications," *The Academy of Management Review* 20, no. 1 (1995): 65–91.
3. Andrew Carnegie is generally credited with creating the term "corporate social responsibility" in his 1889 essay entitled *The Gospel of Wealth.*
4. See Archie B. Carroll, "A Three-Dimensional Conceptual Model of

Corporate Performance," *The Academy of Management Review* 4 (1979):497–505 and Archie B. Carroll, "Corporate Social Responsibility: Evolution of a Definitional Construct," *Business & Society* 38, no. 3 (1999): 268–295.
5. Paine, Lynn S. *Value Shift: Why Companies Must Merge Social and Financial Imperatives to Achieve Superior Performance.* New York: McGraw-Hill, 2003.
6. See *www.americanexpress.com.*
7. See Jean Tirole, "Corporate Governance," *Econometrica* 69, no. 1 (2001): 1–35.

8. Robert Kaplan and David Norton, *The Balanced Scorecard: Translating Strategy into Action*, Harvard Business School Press, 1996.

9. John Elkington, *Cannibals With Forks: The Triple Bottom Line of 21st Century Business,* Capstone Publishing, 1997.

10. Diane Swanson, "Toward an Integrative Theory of Business and Society: A Research Strategy for Corporate Social Performance," *Academy of Management Review, 24* (1999): 506–521.

11. Edgar Schein, *Organizational culture and leadership*, 2nd ed., San Francisco, CA: Jossey-Bass, 1992.

12. Michael Jensen, "Value Maximization, Stakeholder Theory, and the Corporate Objective Function," *Journal of Applied Corporate Finance* 14, no. 3 (2001): 8–21.

13. Data if from *www.sustainability-indexes.com.*

14. Sophia A. Muirhead, Charles J. Bennett, Ronald E. Berenbeim, Amy Kao, and David J. Vidal, *Corporate Citizenship in the New Century: Accountabilility, Transparency, and Global Stakeholder Engagement*, The Conference Board, Research Report # R-1314–02-RR, July 2002.

Index